INVENTING OURSELVES AGAIN
Women Face Middle Age

INVENTING OURSELVES AGAIN
Women Face Middle Age

Janis Fisher Chan

Foreword by Margo Hackett

SIBYL
PUBLICATIONS
Portland, Oregon

Published by **SIBYL Publications** • 600 S.E. Powell Blvd • Portland, Oregon
97202 • (503) 231-6519 • 1-800-240-8566

Editor: *Marge Columbus*
Graphic Design: *Design Studio Selby*

6 5 4 3 2 1

Passages from *Sister Age* by M.F.K. Fisher, © 1983 and *The Second Sex* by Simone de
Beauvoir © 1989 are reprinted by permission of Random House, Inc.

Passages from *Midlife in Perspective* by Herant Katchadourian, M.D. © 1986 are reprinted
by permission of the W.H. Freeman Company.

Passages from *Journal of a Solitude* by May Sarton © 1973, *At Seventy: A Journal* by May
Sarton © 1984, and *The House by the Sea: A Journal* by May Sarton © 1977 are reprinted
by permission of W.W. Norton & Company.

Quotes by Grace Slick in an article by D'Arcy Fallon are reprinted with permission from
the *San Francisco Examiner* © 1989 *San Francisco Examiner*.

Cataloging in Publication Data

Chan, Janis Fisher
    Inventing Ourselves Again : women face midlife / by Janis
Fisher Chan.
    p. cm.
    ISBN 0-9638327-1-9

    1. Middle aged women--Psychology. 2. Middle aged women--
Attitudes. 3. Middle age--Psychological aspects. I. Title.
HQ1059.4.C43 1996   305.24'4'082
                         QBI96-20448

Printed and bound in the United States of America

To my mother, who has found the strength to invent herself again.

CONTENTS

FOREWORD

To me, this book is about intimacy, courage, and possibilities. I have always loved the sound of women's voices telling stories. I remember lying next to my mother on her bed as she spoke to friends on the telephone. Imagining myself on the other end of the line, I'd make up my own story and lie there, contented, for hours. The same thing happened to me when I read these pages. I picked up the dialogue and entered into the conversations.

Inventing Ourselves Again affirms the juiciness of a woman's life at an age when we had expected all the juice to be gone. Now that I'm at that age myself, it delights me to discover that I'll be licking the sweetness off my chin for quite some time.

When Janis Chan asked to interview me, I was surprised. I knew she wrote, but I didn't realize she was writing a book. I had assumed that only an "author" could write a book, and it had never occurred to me that someone I knew could be an author. But after I read the manuscript (which I did in two big gulps), I cried. I cried because the book was over and I wanted it to go on forever. It had told me with precise tenderness who we are and what we feel and what we know. And as I thought about what I had read, something essential happened: I developed the confidence to write a book of my own.

I hope that when you, too, read *Inventing Ourselves Again*, you realize that your place in the world is not getting smaller, but brighter. I hope that you sit with your friends on a gray afternoon and whisper and laugh and cry. That you encourage each other with your talk and your stories. Because when women talk to each other—and when we tell each other our stories—magic things can happen. We can transform isolation into possibility and fear into a strong embrace.

—MARGO HACKETT
Berkeley, California

PROLOGUE

This book began as a personal journal, an attempt to make sense of the changes in my body and my psyche as I approached my fiftieth birthday. I quickly noticed that the themes in my conversations with myself were also coming up in conversations with my friends, wonderful conversations in which we explored our most intimate concerns, fears, discoveries, and dreams. I kept trying to recapture those conversations in my journal. I was fascinated by the way in which my generation of women, who had been raised to consider other women competitors in the game of life, had learned to share with and support one another. Here we were, doing it again, helping each other into and through a midlife that is unlike anything we could have imagined for ourselves.

The women whose voices are included in this book were not selected in any scientific way. They are my friends and acquaintances; two are my cousins. We are not baby boomers; we are their older sisters. Five of us were raised on the West Coast; the others are from Kansas and New Jersey and Michigan and New York and Montreal, although all but one has lived in California for most of her adult life. Most, but not all, of us are the children or grandchildren of immigrants. Most of us have college degrees, and most of us have always worked at least part-time. Some of us are professionals; some are artists. All but two of us have grown children; all but three have been divorced or never married.

As I talked with each woman, I loved the interplay of our reflections and feelings and ideas and discoveries. I loved the themes that kept coming up over and over: Midlife is a time of great learning and great opportunity. As we talked, I also saw that because we have so few role models, we are doing what we've always done: Finding our way as we go along, creating new ways of growing older. I hope our discoveries can be as exciting and useful to other women as they are to us.

THE WOMEN

Sachiko: A dancer and choreographer raised in Oakland, now lives in San Francisco. Co-founder of the Asian America Dance Collective and performs her own work nationwide. Married a second husband eight years ago and has one stepdaughter.

Vivian: An educator, raised in Los Angeles, and a longtime resident of Marin County. Married, with three adult children, she recently became a grandmother. As a learning disabilities specialist, she designed and implemented programs for low-income children in Marin City and now runs her own consulting business.

Anita: An attorney and judge, raised in Los Angeles, who has lived in Orange County for most of her adult life. She is married and has three adult children.

Judy: A businesswoman who was raised on the San Francisco Peninsula and has lived in the East Bay for many years. Divorced, she has two adult children and one grandson.

Melva: A human resources officer, raised in Kansas, and lives in Oakland. Divorced with two adult children.

Maureen: A legal secretary, raised in Montreal, who moved to San Francisco in the mid-Sixties. She has lived in Marin County for many years. She's divorced and has two children in college.

Lynn: A copy editor and proofreader who was raised in Michigan and has lived in Marin County for many years. She never married and has two grown children.

Leslie: A freelance magazine copy editor who was raised in New Jersey where she now lives again after fifteen years in the San Francisco Bay Area. She has three adult children by her first marriage and one teenage daughter by her current husband.

Margo: A former poncho saleswoman and arts administrator, raised in New York and Tucson, who has lived in Berkeley with her second husband since the early 1970s. She is now writing a book on women in Paris. No children.

Susan: An executive recruiter who was raised in New York and now lives in Marin County. In the early Seventies, she moved on her own with two young daughters, now grown, to San Francisco. She is divorced.

Marlene: The executive director of YWCAs in three metropolitan areas for ten years, she is now development director for a private high school. Raised in Nebraska, she now lives in the East Bay. She plays violin with a chamber group. She is divorced, with two grown daughters.

Betty: A professor and former chair of a university Native American Studies department. She was born and raised in Alaska, and earned her graduate degree from Harvard. She is divorced with three grown children.

GROWING UP IS HARD TO DO

NOT WHAT I'D EXPECTED

Fifty looks settled, it looks answered, it looks finished, it looks ... grown up. Fifty is not a time when you would have doubts about yourself, or would still be changing. Turning fifty is something my mother did, not anything I'm ready for because I'm not grown up yet. So how can you be not a grownup and fifty at the same time?

—Susan

What does being in your fifties mean if it doesn't mean growing up, becoming at last the adult human being you are expected to become? Maybe it's impossible to become a grownup much before fifty, unless you have worked hard at discovering and accepting who you are, at reconciling the paradoxes in your life, at learning to recognize success and live with disappointment and unhappiness and loss and failure, at finding ways to be detached and objective without disconnecting, and experiencing every moment fully without losing your sense of where you are in time and space, of what's gone by and what's still to come. At learning to take responsibility for yourself and to do what you can for others.

This is a dream I had last night. I was in a perfectly wide open house, a big wide open space. No walls or bars, but I couldn't get out. And voices, and people being able to find me wherever I was. It was clear imprisonment, even though there was no prison. And when I woke up, I was in my room alone, screaming. I thought it was a metaphor for smoking. But now I think it has to do with being trapped

in a place in which I no longer belong. Do you off-load
everything? Or is this really a time when you open the
door? I built my own prison; there are no bars, there are
no windows, I know I can walk out. But am I willing to go?

—*Susan*

But wouldn't it be nice to be able to go out the door and
leave the door open, so you could come back …

And not view it as a prison …

Now I'm ready to walk. I may not go more than a few yards
today, but I'll go a few yards out and see what the world is like in
this direction, and I'll come back …

That's so grown up. Knowing the balance is there, and
relying on the balance to be there. You gotta believe it's
there and get rid of the impatience.

"You've got to get rid of the impatience." At fifty-four I finally understand. Impatience defines youth, not age. We've already done impatience. We are already quite familiar, thank you,
with the unbearable ache of having to wait for something we can't
live without, for Christmas finally to come, for the cute boy in
home room to ask for a date, for the day of graduation from an
eternity of school. To get a real job. To get married. For the first
baby to be born. We no longer need impatience. What we need,
what we're finally learning how to do, is to slow down and make
conscious choices. To allow ourselves to take risks, knowing they
are risks, knowing what we risk. Yesterday we reached for extremes;
now we strive for balance. We are willing to not have it all, because we see that that's the only way we'll get anything.

And time has become a real factor. We don't have that much
time left. If we risk everything, take too deep a plunge, we may

not have time to swim back to the surface. If things don't work out, do we have time to recover and start again? Old bones mend slowly, or not at all. Being grown up also means realizing that achieving "it" is not so important after all. By now we should know that when we do get "there," it's not usually what we'd expected. By now we should know that it's the journey that's important.

> *"Grown up" was to us the white gloves and the perfect behavior and the house with the picket fence. But grown up has nothing to do with all that. It has to do with being responsible for your own creation. I'm responsible for me. Of all the things I've come to, that's the one I enjoy the most. Because it's the most powerful. If I've created it, I can uncreate it, change it. I'm like a mad inventor. And that's why the next twenty years is so important. Because I never realized that I was inventing myself all this time.*
>
> *—Susan*

Until I was almost fifty, I assumed that I would become a grownup at some clearly defined point in my life. I would not be a grownup for a long time, and then I would be one, and I would know. But the older I got, the fuzzier the word became, like a word drawn by a skywriter in a summer sky. The older I got, the more the concept of "grownup" changed from absolute and real to abstract, meaningless, an idea meant to fool children into behaving properly.

Now I feel silly for not having realized the obvious: You find no clear moment when you are transformed into a grownup, the way a larva is transformed into a butterfly and emerges from its cocoon knowing that it is an adult. It doesn't happen automatically when you graduate from high school, as I once thought. It doesn't happen just because you turn twenty-one, get a job, get married, take out a mortgage, become a mom, or do any of those other "grownup" things. You don't make it happen by abandoning blue jeans for tailored suits, trimming your hair, remembering to cross your legs at the ankle instead of the knee, developing perfect posture, or learning to set a perfect table. It happens slowly, over time. Just as you slowly evolved from a helpless infant into an adult capable of managing your own life and healing your own hurts, you slowly evolve into as much of a grownup as you are ever going to be.

And now that I finally believe that I *have* become a grownup, it isn't what I'd expected. I think I'd expected ...

financial security	a perfect house
gentility	sexlessness
invisibility	wisdom
authority	knowledge
a predictable future	a fixed point of view
the end of experimentation	

What I've found is:

more patience	more knowledge
less time	uncertainty
more self-acceptance	more contentment
more self-confidence	more fear about the
an enduring sexuality	future
some loneliness	unwelcome physical
less interest in things	changes
more caution	a longing for solitude
more resistance to change	a need to experiment
a need for change	a need for challenges

*There's a real price you pay for putting responsibility on
someone else: "My mother did this to me." You get stuck.*

—Judy

More than anything, being a grownup means being responsible to and for yourself—and at the same time, sharing the responsibility for others. You understand what responsibility means,
recognize the importance of choices, actions, and inactions. You
know what is possible and what is not, accepting limitations while
being willing to challenge them, knowing you might not succeed
or that success might be different from what you envisioned. You
understand, *know*, that you are the person who is responsible for
you. You can stop blaming your mother, your father, your big
brother, your first husband, your boss, the Republicans, the "others," for everything you don't like about your life. You can be angry at the people who let you down, or put you down, recognize
that you've had bad breaks and your life might have been different *if only* … and at the same time accept reality as reality and
move on. You can't be a grownup and a victim at the same time.
The two states of mind are mutually exclusive.

"Grownup" *is* a state of mind, a point of view that shifts as
easily as the wind. Some days, I feel myself to be a grownup, without question, especially in my relationships. For instance, I've always been a grownup to my children. I know things they don't, I
make decisions with (apparent) confidence, and I'm always ready
with advice they don't want but know they need about everything from lovers to apartment leases to budgets to bosses to birth
control. Amazingly, I've also become a grownup in the eyes of my
own parents. As they've aged and become frail, they have begun
to see me as a competent (!), reliable, responsible, knowledgeable
person to whom they can turn for support in time of need.

Although … you never, ever stop being your parents' child.

From my journal, eighteen months before my fiftieth birthday:

I am planning my parents' fiftieth wedding anniversary party and my father knows I am going to screw it up. No matter that I have successfully raised two children, run several businesses, never been arrested, never gone insane, stayed married to the same person for over two decades, and have money in the bank. I am his daughter and incapable of doing anything right.

"Don't you think you'd better find a place?"

"I'm working on it, Dad."

"There's not much time."

"Don't worry about it, Dad." I mention that we may not be able to come to dinner the night before the party.

"Typical," he says.

"What does that mean?" I counter before thinking.

"Typical of you," he says. "You never make up your mind until the last minute."

This is me, Dad, I want to shout, the most organized person anyone knows. Who do you think found the perfect caterer? The perfect place? Made sure her little brother sent the invitations out on time? And all you can say is, "Typical."

Mom and Dad turned eighty last year. I was fortunate to enter my middle years with two independent parents with whom I could finally talk honestly, truthfully, adult to adult. Yet once I had the chance to settle all the burning issues that haunted me through my twenties and thirties, even into my forties, they no longer mattered much. Most of that unfinished business seemed to have melted away like the last tendrils of fog on an October morning. My parents had grown old, and I had become a grownup. I felt no need to burden them with the unfinished business that still gnawed at my psyche and would now remain unfinished unless I chose to finish it myself. It turns out that I learned something I never thought I'd learn: To accept my mother and father as they are, to accept the way we relate to one another, and to appreciate the good parts and forget the parts I once longed to change. After all, I am a grownup now and can take care of myself.

Anyway, it's useless for a woman in her mid-fifties to wilt when her father snaps at her. Useless.

AVOIDING THE GROWNUP BOX

Jeez, I feel like I'm a hundred million years old. Here we are; we're getting into our fifties, and where are these people who keep coming to our shows coming from? What do they find so fascinating about these middle-aged bastards playing ... the same thing we've always played? (Jerry Garcia, *San Francisco Chronicle* "Datebook," October 27, 1991)

Fifty is something that happened to my parents and their friends. They were ready for it, and they looked it and acted it.

—*Susan*

"Middle-aged rock star." It's an oxymoron. "Graybeards." The way I learned it, rock music is a revolution against the reasonable, responsible grownups who control your world until you bust out in adolescence. I expected my parents to hate my music. (My mother still complains when I pick up an oldies-but-goodies station: "How can you listen to that junk?") It came as no surprise that my musician father scoffed at the Beatles' "Hard Day's Night" as nothing but noise (although years later he admitted he could finally hear the music). Rock music was ours, and it set us apart.

But now that middle age is happening to us, we find we're not ready; we don't look it and we're not acting it. In her late forties, former Jefferson Airplane singer Grace Slick returned to the stage to the acclaim of rock fans of all ages, while her daughter, China Kantner, my children's contemporary, became a rock 'n' roll deejay on MTV. People old, young, and in-between trail the Grateful Dead around the country. Graying, paunchy parents hoot and stamp their feet alongside their kids at rock concerts. At a friend's fiftieth birthday party, the fifteen-year-old son manages the stereo while we middle-aged moms and dads swing our spreading hips to music so loud you have to lip-read to have a conversation.

I'm very aware not to act like a teenager, oh, I'm so young and hip. But I feel able to be who I am and relate to younger people. It's more of a credit to them than to me. I think these kids are exceedingly sophisticated and comfortable with adults—that's one thing we didn't do at that age. I was very uptight with parents.

—Leslie

Are our kids surprised, or amused, to find that their parents understand and even share their love of rock? It probably seems natural to them. After all, they were weaned on the Beatles and the Rolling Stones. Maybe they never have seen us in quite the same way we saw our parents, as grownups with boring, predictable lives and a predilection for scowling at anything they didn't understand. I've always liked to think that I have a stronger connection with my children than my parents had with me. I've been pleased when they talked to me about things I'd never in a million years have mentioned to my parents, like sex and drugs and peer pressure. I wanted them to see me the way I saw my slightly eccentric aunt Dot, the one person in the family who didn't seem to be a real grownup, the person I could talk to about anything, the person with whom I could be myself. But it's always a balancing act. No matter how cool you want to be, you are still the parent, and sometimes you have to be the grownup who says "no" and sets limits. And sometimes they have to be the kids who keep secrets and protect Mom and Dad from things that would only upset them.

> I was brought up speaking French, and you say "tu" and "vous." I'd say "tu" to my cousins, to my brothers and sisters. But to all my aunts and my parents, I've always said, "vous." I would never dare say "tu" to my parents. In my house, there's no line between parent and child. We're all equal. It makes it harder. There's less respect, really. If I were to do it again, I would be more of a disciplinarian, not much, but a little.
>
> —Maureen

My almost-grownup children say that as teenagers, they were glad to have parents who understood their angst and their need to experiment. They seem comfortable discussing with us the ins and outs of young adulthood. I welcome those intimate conversations and try to listen actively instead of immediately presenting solutions and advice. I would like to think that my children are beginning to see me as a friend. But I must continually remind myself that even though they might accept me as a sometime friend, they still need and want me mostly to be a grownup. Mom who occasionally forgets herself and scowls at their clothes, showers them with unwanted advice, demands that they pick up after themselves when they're home for an overnight or a few months. Mom who cares enough to remind them to be responsible about drinking and drugs and sex and money. Mom who loves them unconditionally and will always try her damnedest to protect them, even when it's not possible. We may have blurred the line between parent and child by refusing to stay in the grownup box all the time, by smoking a little pot, going to rock concerts, and taping our kids' CDs to play in the car. But we're the parents and they're the kids, until they've grown up and figured out all the life lessons we've taken so long to learn. Or that we take such pleasure in thinking we've learned.

JUST ANOTHER AWKWARD STAGE

I like to think of all of us sitting in our rocking chairs at age ninety in Mendocino or some place, smoking a little dope and playing a little Go, and talking politics, maybe going out dancing.

—*Leslie*

I think I see myself as an irascible old lady at some point. Having flown in the face of convention most of my life, I will indeed be able to fly very high in the face of convention.

—*Susan*

When my friends and I talk about women we admire, we name unconventional women we find interesting precisely because of their eccentricities. When we talk about getting old, we joke about becoming those eccentric little old ladies. Respectable little old ladyhood doesn't interest us at all. We're not going to be quiet, demure, conventional old ladies everyone takes care of and ignores. My personal game plan is to be an extremely weird old lady. I want my children and grandchildren to shake their heads and cluck their tongues and whisper about me. "What are we going to do about Mom? What in the world is she going to do next?" I want people to wonder about me and admire me and gossip about me. I want women in their forties and fifties to look at me with admiration and say, "*That's* what I want to be like when I'm old!"

There's something to be said for growing old gracefully, but it's easier for young people to say it.

—*Melva*

The immediate problem is not how to handle being old. It's how to handle the in-between years, all that time before I'm old enough to be considered admirably eccentric. Because who's interested in an eccentric *middle-aged* lady? All you can say about eccentric middle-aged ladies is that you're glad they're not *your* mother.

From my journal a few months before I turned fifty:

> *The mail brings brochures for publications I've seen only in my parents' house.* Modern Maturity *and its ilk. Addressed to me? What can they be thinking of? Me, the Mature Woman? I throw the brochures in the trash, ashamed that someone might see them. They make me uneasy. And yet. And yet. What are we going to be like, this odd generation that has begun to move (gracefully or otherwise) through middle age into seniorhood? After all, we are the kids who marched against the Vietnam War, who flaunted authority, smoked dope in Golden Gate Park, garbed our firstborn in tie-dyed T-shirts. We are getting old, damn it, and we're not even sure what that means.*

Middle age is one of those awkward in-between times, another of those frustrating developmental stages when you're no longer one thing but not yet another. It reminds me unpleasantly of adolescence, in fact, that eternity when my body kept surprising and betraying me, when every morning brought a different mood, when much of the time I felt like a changeling abandoned by mistake among a race of beings who looked and behaved in unfathomable ways. That's exactly what's happening to me now. My body keeps surprising and betraying me. Every morning brings a different mood. Some days I feel that I have been abandoned among aliens who expect me to look and behave like an odd creature called "Middle-aged Woman." Who *is* this woman? She's not old, but she is clearly no longer young, either. She's stuck in the middle, caught once again in the process of becoming. Like an adolescent, she wants desperately to belong, but all too often she feels uncomfortable and out of place.

One of these days, I suppose, I'll relax into my middle-aged self. I'll even find things about this stage of life that are pleasing to me. Of course, as soon as I settle in, as soon as I allow myself to relax and become complacent, the aliens will knock me off balance again by expecting me to look and behave like yet another odd creature, "Elderly Woman." But I won't mind. I finally understand that the aliens serve an important purpose. For me, complacency is a living death, and being knocked off balance from time to time, however difficult and unpleasant, is essential to my ability to learn and grow. So I'm preparing myself. I'm planning to display my wrinkles like badges, trade my increasingly tight jeans for a nice loose mother hubbard (tie-dyed, of course), and relax into eccentricity. Come to think of it, I can hardly wait.

"THIS IS WHAT FIFTY *LOOKS* LIKE!"
—Gloria Steinem

*The first time I really noticed it was at work. It was my
birthday, and the cake was out and everybody was standing around. And one man, about thirty, asked me how old
I was. And I said forty-six. And his response ... I don't
remember the words, but his voice was so patronizing ...
the way I'd be to an old lady who was ninety-five, so
amazed that they're so old and still doing so well. And I
thought, oh shit.*

—Marlene

Certain characteristics define us in other people's eyes, although not always in our own. Gender, for one. I read once that
the one thing you remember about someone you've met even
briefly is whether the person was male or female, and I've found
that to be true. You probably remember someone's ethnicity and
whether he or she is your countryperson. In the same way, you
remember a person's age. Possibly not the real age, but the age he
or she appears to be: "Young, old, about my age, in her twenties,
her thirties. About my mother's age."

*I think the first time I realized I was getting older was
when I went to see a new doctor and the man was ... a
child. I thought, well, how does he know anything? And
that was a long time ago. But I refuse to experience the
difference in perception that the world has of me as an
older woman. I'm not an older person! It's funny, but it's
on some level true. Having had my fourth child at forty-*

one, I'm still doing the same things. I've Peter Panned myself. People are always surprised to find out how old I am. Until two or three years ago people didn't believe it. Now they're beginning to believe it. Damn it.

—Leslie

For me, the first glimmer of "Oh my God I'm getting old" was when I became aware of a difference in the way other people behaved towards me ...

Like you're thinking you're thirty, and then someone treats you with respect or distance ...

—Vivian

Or as if you're invisible. People's eyes float over you or move away quickly as they fit you into a slot: "Ah, it's only a middle-aged woman, a person of no consequence, not worth acknowledging."

I've felt that being a woman, and I've felt that being short. Another odd thing is in terms of relating to women and relating to men. It's funny for me to think that a thirty-year-old man would think of me as a fifty-year-old woman.

But you certainly don't look like a fifty-year-old woman, I say. We laugh. "But then, who does?"

People can't believe I'm fifty. I have a lot of arguments about that. People are shocked when they find out how old my children are. It's kind of neat. It gives me kind of a rush to think that I am fifty but don't look fifty to people. But it has a flip side, like, my God, what's the matter with me?

—Betty

When I was still a few months shy of fifty, I was in a South of Market cafe with several people in their twenties and early thirties. My age came up in conversation. After a discernible moment of silence, one woman laughed uncomfortably and said, "Oh, I thought you were about forty or something." Someone made an unrelated joke and everyone relaxed. Sort of. Three or four months later, I mentioned to a forty-year-old man I'd known for years that my husband had thrown me a wonderful fiftieth birthday party. His eyes widening, he blurted, "I didn't know you were *that* old!" I didn't know what to say. "Thanks, I needed that today." "Well, now you know." "I lied. I'm only thirty-three."

I admit that when someone expresses surprise at my age, I feel a flash of pleasure. I want people to think of me as younger. At the same time, I feel a certain anger. Why should other people feel embarrassed because *I'm* middle-aged? Why should I feel embarrassed? I've seen a less emotional response to the discovery that someone had a criminal record or been caught *delicto in flagrante*. It's ridiculous to feel you should apologize for your age. "I'm so sorry I'm getting old. Perhaps you'd be happier if I hadn't made it quite so far."

I'm never going to be that grownup older woman I thought I was going to be. That's me now, and that's not the way I see myself.
—Vivian

I think of myself as young. They say that you kind of fix on an age in your mind and stay there. Mine's thirty-six. And fifty is real far away from thirty-six.
—Melva

But it's not how others see us that's important, it's how we see ourselves.

What did I think I'd be like at fifty? Like other people I'd seen in magazines. Somebody's mother. Not me as a mother. My hair would be gray. I would be rounder. Less active, physically and mentally, certainly less energetic. Content to cook Thanksgiving dinners for my family who would be happy to come and eat them. I'd wear an apron and sensible shoes. I'd drive a sensible car. Maybe I wouldn't drive. Certainly not sexy. Certainly not a vital woman. That's the surprise. I feel very much like a vital woman. I don't know if I strike anyone else that way. But it's how I feel inside of me, and how I expect people should react back to me.

—Vivian

Not only does it strike me odd that people react to me in a certain way just because I am a certain age, I make mistakes about people's ages in relationship to my own. Sometimes I assume that a person is about my age, only to discover he or she is several years younger. In the same way, when I meet or hear about someone close to my age, I often think of the person as "older." Listening to a discussion on National Public Radio about Senator Sam Nunn's retirement, I was shocked to learn that he is only two years older than I am. After all, he's been in Congress forever.

I make those mistakes because of my own mental image of a middle-aged woman.

Which is what? Vivian asks.

Not me!

Exactly!

When I was a child, if I thought of someone who was fifty, I would have thought of someone pretty old with gray hair and a cane. And a rocking chair. Probably knitting sweaters for grandkids. Or being an old maid and doting on her

nieces and nephews. Someone who was neat and clean
and tidy and did flower arrangements. I never had grand-
parents, so that image comes from someplace else.

—*Sachiko*

For me, the word "middle-aged" conjures up specific images,
including: stout walking shoes, tweed hats, little felt hats with
veils, black and navy blue suits on square bodies, thick hose, beige
silk blouses with pearls, afternoon tea, print house dresses with
aprons, tight permanent waves, glasses on neck chains, four-door
American sedans, very clean, clip-on rhinestone earrings, polyester pants suits with plastic sandals, lap dogs.

Where in the world did those images of a middle-aged woman
come from? My mother, who turned fifty when I was in my mid-
twenties and not paying attention, had short, stylish dark brown
hair with reddish highlights. (She kept that hair into her early
seventies, when a kindly hairdresser hinted that it might be time
to reveal her natural gray.) She never, to my knowledge, drank
afternoon tea, or wore any kind of hat, or had a lap dog. She did
not own a pair of stout walking shoes. She did occasionally wear
clip-on rhinestone earrings—which I borrowed for my senior prom.
She did drive an immaculate four-door Hudson the size of a small
tank and preferred polyester slacks because they didn't wrinkle.
All that had far less to do with being middle-aged than with living during the 1950s.

Still, Mom was always "Mom," and to me, the word meant
"old."

"I don't think I have my finger on the pulse as much as
some people. I'm kind of out of it ... I don't go to clubs."

"Are you saying you're getting old?"

"I don't know. I do know that the roughest thing in the world is to be an older woman ... In my mind, my mother is an older woman. She's 65 and I'm 45, but I don't think of myself that way. I don't know what I am supposed to base myself on—how I look, how I feel, how many years I have? When do I have to cut my hair and quit wearing jeans and my leather jacket and going on motorcycle rides? When do I have to start wearing a bun and stay home? (Cher on Men, Music and Film, San Francisco Chronicle "Date-book," December 8, 1991)

Though our images of middle age have little to do with the real thing, we still think that by the time we're in our fifties we will have changed the way we look, the way we dress, the way we behave. In spite of the evidence around us, we believe that middle-aged women don't wear tight jeans and T-shirts with slogans unless they want to look like middle-aged eccentrics, that they don't laugh too loud or otherwise call attention to themselves, that people will apologize for swearing in their presence and be careful not to tell them dirty jokes.

Occasionally I ... realize that any ... spiritual upset brought about by my serving an exotic or eccentric dish would do more harm than good, and I bow. It is usually women past middle age who thus confound me ... Perhaps it is not too late ... perhaps the next time ... I will blast their safe tidy little lives with a big tureen of hot borscht and some garlic toast and salad, instead of the "fruit cocktail," fish, meat, vegetable, salad, dessert, and coffee they tuck daintily away seven times a week ... (M. F. K. Fisher, The Gastronomical Me)

*But here where we live, today, fifty-year-old ladies don't
have gray hair and little old lady clothes. It would be interesting to see what it's like to be fifty somewhere else.*

—*Vivian*

Vivian and I live in northern California, in affluent, progressive, liberal Marin County, home to peacock feathers and com-
munal hot tubs. My friends and I do not represent the average
American woman—if there is such a being. But we are typical of
the educated middle-class women who are flexing their intellec-
tual and political muscles all over the country. I've seen us in Seattle, Los Angeles, Tucson, Washington, D.C., Santa Fe, and
Mendham, New Jersey; I've run into us on the streets of London,
Paris, Madrid, Hong Kong, and Beijing. We're finally being seen
on television, in films, on stage, and in magazines (although seldom on the cover). We're in Congress and on the Supreme Court
and in the White House, although our representative in the White
House is taking pains of late to resemble a middle-aged frump
instead of the hip feminist baby boomer we know her to be. Still,
we are not "everywoman." Returning to Oklahoma for a twentieth high school reunion, a friend found her classmates wearing
dowdy (by her standards) dresses and styling their hair in the tight
beauty parlor curls we abandoned decades ago. "They're not even
forty," she told me, "and they look as if they're in their fifties!" To
my friend, "in their fifties" *meant* dowdy dresses and tight beauty
parlor curls. By contrast, most of the closing-in-on-fifty women at
my thirtieth high school reunion on the San Francisco Peninsula
looked as if they had just come from the gym, flush with the bloom
of youth, strong, clear-eyed, fresh-faced, *young*. Certainly not as if
they were a wink shy of *middle-aged*.

But in the face of reality, stereotypes persist, and in our rush to avoid them, we consciously avoid whatever symbolizes "middle age" to us.

> I'm starting to lose my glasses. I'm going to have to wear them with chains, and wearing chains with glasses is for old folks. I refuse to do that. Glasses on a chain symbolize aging more than anything else for me.
>
> —Anita

> When I was young, I thought a fifty-year-old woman was old. Dowdy. Overweight. Wrinkled. Gray hair pulled back in a bun. Glasses. I had enough picture books in my childhood that I knew how Grandmas looked, and Grandma was fifty.
>
> —Marlene

When I evoke my grandmother, she comes to me in a little print dress with pinafore apron, crinkly gray hair and sunken cheeks, bright, dark eyes. "How are you, honey?" she says in a warm and loving voice. She wears hose held up with little elastic garters, even in the summer, and when she sits, I see her bare white flesh above the garters. She wears sensible stout black shoes. I've always hated little print dresses and pinafore aprons and sensible shoes because I knew that wearing them would make me old.

> I understand intellectually what being fifty means, and it doesn't mean whether or not you wear blue jeans on a Sunday afternoon. That doesn't mean anything, but that's straight from my mind, and it has nothing to do with the reality of my person.
>
> —Leslie

On the day I turned fifty, I closed my bedroom door and confronted myself in the mirror. To my surprise, I saw no miraculous transformation. I was the same person, a little slower than at twenty or forty-two, a little heavier, far more calm, much more confident, far more patient. But I was still *me*, first and foremost, not primarily a mom, or a grandma, or an auntie, but *me*, plain and simple. No one was making me turn in my tennis shorts for pinafore aprons, my Nikes for sensible shoes, my Levi 501s for polyester pants suits. No one was forcing me into a corner to sit quietly with my ankles crossed. Nothing had changed—except that everything had changed, because after all those years as a pseudo-adult, I realized that I had finally grown up.

A HISTORICAL PERSPECTIVE

MY LIFE AS HISTORY

The most important things that have happened over my life are medical advances. Like people used to be crippled from polio. I see history as cycles. We've progressed technically, but I think our humanness stays the same. Antony and Cleopatra went through the same stuff. The Bible parallels things that happen today. We don't really learn from things that happen to us as human beings. My kids have to learn the things I've already learned. "Don't do that," I try to tell them. "If you do that ... " And they do it anyway. "I could have told you that." I don't see us as being all that enlightened.

—Melva

From behind the cyclone fence that separates onlookers from the landing strip, I watch my grandfather's face as he escorts my grandmother down the portable stairway. The year is 1948, and my Bubba and Zadie have taken their first airplane flight, up over the Rockies from Sioux City, Iowa, to San Francisco, California. My little brother and I jump and holler and wave, but my grandfather walks slowly, proudly down the rickety steps and across the tarmac, only the sparkling eyes behind his round wire spectacles betraying his excitement. Perhaps he had felt the same excitement, the same pride, as he stood at the rail of the ship that carried him from the Old World to the New, as he sailed across the Atlantic Ocean into New York Harbor, past the Statue of Liberty, to Ellis Island where he would begin a new life in America. Then as now, he had taken an immense journey, and in both journeys he had traversed time as well as space.

Today I understand a little of what my grandfather must have felt. By the time you're in your fifties, you have a *lifetime* to look back on. I examine that eight-year-old me jumping and waving behind the airport fence, skinny and intense with bouncing curls and huge dark eyes, a short plaid skirt, little white socks, and shiny new Mary Janes. She is hard at work, that little girl, at the business of growing up, school and books and toys and games. She has no idea how rapidly the postwar world is changing around her and how those changes will shape her life.

> When I think back, I was born at a momentous moment, three weeks before Pearl Harbor. When we went into Manzanar, I was only a few months old.
>
> —Sachiko

Nearly half a century separates Sachiko from the little girl who was uprooted with her family and sent to live in the desert for no reason other than the color of their skin and the shape of their eyes. Nearly half a century separates me from the little girl who watched her immigrant grandfather proudly escort her immigrant grandmother down the steps of a propeller plane. And while we've been going about the business of our lives, Sachiko and I, those lives have become the history children learn in school.

My children's high school history texts were filled with events that happened about the time I was born and while I myself was in school: World War II, Hitler's march through Europe, the Holocaust, Pearl Harbor, the Japanese occupation of China, the internment of Japanese-Americans in concentration camps, the testing of atomic bombs on the civilian populations of Hiroshima and Nagasaki. The Communist Revolution in China. The Korean War (sorry, "police action"). McCarthy and the Red Menace

("Better Dead than Red"). Brown vs. the Board of Education, grownups stoning children on the streets of Selma. The Kennedy and Nixon debates: politics in your living room, beauty and the beast in black and white, pasty-faced Nixon looking like something dug up out of a crypt, right up there on the screen next to America's heart-throb. Khrushchev at Disneyland. Jack Kennedy assassinated. Martin Luther King Jr. assassinated. Robert Kennedy assassinated. Neil Armstrong landing on the moon ("One small step for *man* ... " [italics added]). The Black Panthers. Vietnam. Vietnam. Vietnam. Children murdered at Kent State. Nixon in China. Watergate. Nixon's resignation. So much has happened.

In my lifetime:

Xerox machines	freeways
condominiums	affirmative action
housing developments	the end of legal segregation
the computer revolution	instant worldwide communi-
four wars	cation on the Internet
the atomic bomb	the Holocaust
the rise and fall of the	the rise and fall of apartheid
Berlin Wall	in South Africa
"ethnic cleansing" (again)	rock music
in Central Europe	rap music
human beings in space	hula hoops
artificial hearts	Frisbees
miniskirts (twice)	beatniks, hippies, yippies,
physical fitness	yuppies, slackers, hackers
sex in the movies	sex on television
television	VCRs
long-play records	45 rpm records
compact disks	fax machines

electric typewriters	Selectric typewriters
computers	cyberspace
synthesized music	stereo sound
jets	widespread use of drugs
motels	politics as ad campaigns
the sexual revolution	AIDS
polio vaccine	penicillin
antibiotics	open heart surgery
organ transplants	widespread air pollution
depletion of the ozone	destruction of the rain forests
cellular phones	Disneyland
Disney World	video games
legalized abortion	birth control pills
contact lenses	silicon implants
collagen implants	life in a test tube
perestroika	the fall of the Soviet Union

and … and … and …

You'd need a crystal ball to pick out the one event, the one change, the one invention that will turn out to have the most profound and long-lasting effects on the future. I thought about that when I visited a "sound installation" set up by an innovative group called the Antenna Theatre in an old barracks at the San Francisco Presidio. Called "Enola Alone," the piece was about the dropping of the first atomic bomb on Hiroshima. You walked through a sequence of stations and listened to the voices of bomber pilots discussing the way they were trained to be emotionally as well as physically distanced from their targets, and you listened to the voices of people who had been in the bomb sites discussing how it felt to be those targets.

The experience swept me back to the Fifties when we were carefully trained (like Pavlov's dogs) to respond to the wail that might signal "bombers on their way," bringing Armageddon to San Carlos, California. Again and again we practiced crouching beneath our desks, arms over our heads, eyes tightly closed to avoid being blinded by the flash of light that would come as the world exploded. With Hiroshima and Nagasaki as models, we learned what happens to your body when you are caught in an atomic blast. I learned my lessons well. Until I was well into my twenties, I had nightmares in which I was not one of those burned to a cinder in the firestorm but a survivor, blind and in pain, vomiting uncontrollably, my skin peeling away as I wandered in shock through the wasteland. My fear was so profound that one winter when I was in college, an unexpected thunder and lightning storm threw me into a panic, and I ran around my apartment looking for some way to kill myself quickly rather than be exposed to a most horrible death. It took several minutes to realize that if the loud noises and bright flashes were really a bomb, I'd already be dead.

I know my nightmares were shared by many people who grew up in the post-World War II world with its hysterical threats of annihilation. But hysterical or not, I know that such annihilation could happen at any time. A deteriorating nuclear power plant could go out of control. A cornered tyrant or crazy terrorist could set off a bomb, triggering an unstoppable chain of events. Our generation is the first to grow up knowing that a careless moment, misdirected anger, paranoia, a *mistake*, could destroy the world. We have had to find a way to live with that; we've done it by keeping ourselves in a state of denial. How else do you live with the knowledge of something so terrifying over which you have no control?

But how different are we, really, from our distant (and not-so-distant) ancestors? Lacking a crystal ball or scientific knowledge, the only way they knew to hold off disaster was to chant certain syllables, or burn witches, or sacrifice their firstborn. Is the fear of atomic destruction much different than the fear that an earthquake will swallow you up or a volcano will bury your village or the crops will fail or the Black Plague will kill your family?

Truly superior beings would recognize the futility of worrying about such things. They would, instead, use their sophisticated technology to improve their plight instead of keeping their heads in the sand and allowing the situation to become increasingly unmanageable. (But then, truly superior beings would never be in such a fix in the first place.) Melva's right. Despite all our technological advances, despite all the lessons readily available from history, we are not enlightened.

So that's our job for the next millennium: Learn to use technology for more than making our lives comfortable, communicating and traveling more rapidly, and waging more deadly wars. We must learn instead how to protect ourselves from accidents and madness, how to save our precious resources and form ourselves into a human community, where we care about and for one another. Then we might become truly superior beings.

CONNECTING BACK

I wasn't instilled with a strong sense of our history, our heritage. I figure I'm the start. I don't connect back. I feel real, real alone, in a sense. On my wall, I have pictures of my grandparents and my great-grandparents, and I know my great-grandparents had been born in slavery, and he looked white and she looked African. He might have been the son of a slave master.

—Melva

One thing that has always struck me is that after the generation that begot you dies, no one knows who you are. You are a sepia photograph hanging on a wall. What was your great-grandmother's name? No one remembers.

—Susan

Four sisters sitting in a row. Three white heads, one an unnatural reddish brown. My mother, Rose, and her baby sister, Marian, giggle over ancient photographs. I see them as they must have been, bursts of child-energy drawing scowls from somber grownups. Marian and Jessie sit so close that their sleeves brush like the leaves of a tree in a soft breeze, yet their eyes never meet. I have seldom heard them speak. On Jessie's left, Dee looks towards the camera but does not seem to see it. She wears a faintly distracted air, as if anxious about being so far from home. Does she suspect that she will pass away in less than two years, the first of my parents' generation to go (except for Uncle Hymie, my mother's older brother, who died twenty or thirty years ago and left the family a long time before that)?

Four sisters sitting in a row. Marian, the baby, is the keeper of the family lore, the one who knows the stories. My Bubba and Zadie, the maternal grandparents I knew only from brief visits, frown stiffly from the walls of her den, surrounded by sepia-toned pictures, Russia in the late 1800s, my great-grandparents, great-aunts, and great-uncles, dressed in their best, holding their breath as the camera performs its miracle.

I'd always heard that my mother was a flirt, pretty and vivacious, the one the boys came to see at the large brick house my grandfather built in Sioux City when his grocery store was prospering, long before its failure during the Depression forced this proudly independent man to work for others. Now I see it. In her late seventies, Rose still dyes her hair. Jessie is the businesswoman, smart and ambitious. Born fifty years later, she would have been an attorney like her daughter, or perhaps a CEO. Whenever I did something my mother didn't like, she would mutter that I was "just like Jessie." Not like Dee, kind and generous and earthy, the only sister who wasn't taken care of but had to work all her life because she married a dreamer. Dee graduated from high school a National Merit Scholar, but she never had the chance to discover what she might have been; money was tight, so only the boy, Uncle Hymie, was given the chance to go to school, and he threw it away. Dee inherited Bubba's sunny disposition, along with her recipes and love of cooking.

Four sisters in a row, four elderly women from Sioux City, the children of Russian Jewish immigrants, the first of the family to be raised as Americans, free from persecution, free from want even during difficult times. They were the first women in their family to be educated, at least through high school. The first to have long lives with leisure time, even Dee. The first to feel confident that their children would, barring accidents, survive their childhoods.

Four sisters in a row. As the cameras flash, I wonder how they see their lives, how it feels to watch their daughters and granddaughters take advantage of opportunities they did not have, just as they took advantage of opportunities not available to their mothers and aunts and grandmothers. I wonder whether they consider how vastly different each generation's lives have been.

My mother was born in the Sacramento Delta. My father came here in the Twenties. He was a second son. His older brother inherited all the property. One of my dad's uncles who was very wealthy adopted Dad and brought him and his wife to the States. Then the stock market crashed, and my dad's uncle wasn't wealthy any more, and that's when my dad become a gardener. Then his wife died and he sent his kids back to Japan. My dad never talked about it. I only found out because my older brother, my half-brother, told me.
—Sachiko

It's hard to believe that I am only the second generation born in this country. It's been only one hundred years, twice the span of my life, since my grandparents left Eastern Europe. I know so little about them, and next to nothing about the families from which they came. Just as my life would have been unimaginable to my great-grandmother, her life is unimaginable to me.

So much change, so quickly. Like many third-generation Americans, especially on the West Coast where people came to forget their past, I have little sense of who I am supposed to be. I knew that my grandparents left "the Old Country" in search of a better life, to escape discrimination and worse, but I never knew the details because they never talked about their lives in the Old

Country or about the journey to America. I knew I was a hyphen-ated American, a Jewish-American, or an American Jew, but apart from sporadic Sunday School attendance and arguments with my mother about going to church with my friends (I sometimes did), and, later, about dating Jewish boys (I didn't), I never knew what being Jewish meant. My family didn't celebrate the Jewish holi-days; we had a Christmas tree and my brother and I exchanged Easter eggs with our friends. My grandfather read a newspaper with strange writing, spoke Yiddish with my grandmother when they didn't want us to know what they were saying, and sometimes went to "schul," but all that had nothing to do with me.

Several years ago I attended the Bat Mitzvah of a friend's daughter in a small Conservative temple in San Francisco. I sat with my friend Barbara, whose parents were Jewish and who had also long abandoned any pretense of being religious. Scattered among the invited guests sat members of the congregation, mostly elderly, their dark, drab clothing in stark contrast to our bright silk blouses and flowered scarves. As the ceremony, which I did not understand, progressed, my attention was drawn from the cel-ebrant to the congregants. Barbara and I had come to the temple the way we would go to a wedding, bright and cheerful, to demon-strate friendship and support. The members of the congregation had come to pray. As they prayed, their murmuring and keening touched a chord in me, some long-forgotten racial memory per-haps, some awareness that extended back beyond the few con-tacts I had with the sanitized Reform Judaism of my youth. I turned to my friend. Before I could whisper my thoughts, Barbara said quietly, "Some part of me belongs here, don't you feel it?"

*My parents, my grandparents, didn't talk about our his-
tory. And I had just read* Beloved *and I called my mom,
and she said, "We didn't ask. They didn't talk about it."*

—Melva

A few years ago, in a last-ditch effort to gather information
about my family before it was too late, I began pulling out my tape
recorder whenever I was with my older relatives. I'm sure I made a
nuisance of myself with all my questions: Did your mother talk
about what it was like for a woman in the Old Country? How did
Grandpa get the money to come to America? What work did
Great-Grandpa do? How did your parents meet? Did your mother
ever vote? What did you do for fun when you were a kid? What
was the Depression like? What happened to all the aunts and uncles
and cousins who stayed? I suspect they enjoyed the attention, as
well as the chance to reminisce. I also have no doubt that they
edited what they told me—or maybe they were editing their own
memories.

Except for Uncle Hymie, I managed to interview all my parents' siblings at least once, including Aunt Dee a few months before her death. By asking questions, often the same questions over
and over, I've been able to piece together something of the lives
of the generation born in this country. I know quite a lot about
being young in Sioux City and San Francisco. I've seen something of my grandparents through their children's eyes. "My father was the most stubborn man in the world," my mother says
again and again. "When he said something, that was it ... but he
was a *good* man, Janis. A good man." I've learned that my father's
father, Grandpa, was a bit of an adventurer who moved his young
family halfway across country because California offered more
opportunity. (It took some doing to convince my grandmother to

leave her friends and family in Lincoln, Nebraska. She only agreed when Grandpa agreed to move her piano.) I know that my mother's mother, my Bubba, was "Grandma" to all the neighborhood children, her house always open and her kitchen filled with good things to eat, and my mother's father, who I called Zadie, was a Socialist who carried local farmers on the grocery store books. I've heard about the union meetings Grandpa held in his cleaning shop while my grandmother and father and aunts slept in two cramped rooms upstairs and streetcars clattered down 24th Street. I know how my parents met. I know a lot.

But so much has been lost. My grandparents were gone long before I felt the urge to connect back. (You don't think of such things when you're twenty-five and immortal.) And when I ask my parents and their sisters about their grandparents in Russia and Romania, or how it was for their parents to travel by ship across the ocean to the land of opportunity, I hit a blank wall: "I don't know, Janis. We never asked." It's as if my grandparents' lives started when they set foot in America. And how can I, safe and warm and free in my middle-class suburban home, blame them for not wanting to talk about the poverty and pogroms they left behind, for wanting to start fresh, to become Americans, and raise American children? "Dis is a vonderful country," my Zadie used to say. "Vonderful."

To my dismay, I do not come from a family of storytellers. Natural storytellers find their experiences so interesting that they seldom stop to think about whether other people want to hear them; they tell the stories again and again, expanding and embellishing them to keep them fresh. But except for Aunt Marian, who talks all the time and makes things up if she doesn't know, my relatives are shy about talking about themselves. They have to be convinced that other people are interested before they are willing to talk. Before they are willing to remember.

When I was in my mid-twenties, I brought my friends Craig and Zilla to my parents' house for dinner. Grandma had died a few years before, and my grandfather had reluctantly moved in with my parents. After dinner, Craig began asking Grandpa about his life. Before I knew it, my grandfather was telling stories about working his way from Romania to the seacoast, about the journey across the ocean to New York, about making his way to Nebraska, where he apprenticed himself to an uncle and learned the cleaning trade. I was astounded. I had never before heard the stories Grandpa told that night. But Craig was interested; he wanted to know. His gentle, probing questions and his obvious respect encouraged my grandfather to remember and to talk about what he remembered.

Someday, I imagine, my grandchildren will ask about my life. At least, I hope they will. I hope they will be interested in what it was like to grow up in the Fifties, to live in Haight-Ashbury in the Sixties, to drive an internal combustion automobile, to work on a computer that took up half the desk, to travel for fifteen hours to reach the Far East, to experience the sweeping political and social changes that took place in the last half of the twentieth century. But to find out what my life has been like, they'll have to ask. Storytelling doesn't come easily to me. I like to talk, but I need help getting started. I'll need them to ask, "Grandma, what was it like when … " "Grandma, tell me more about … "

In a hundred years? All new people. (Anne Lamott, *All New People: A Novel*)

Only one hundred years, and so many changes. The trip to this country took my grandparents many harsh weeks jammed into steerage on an ocean steamer and separated them from their families forever. Today's immigrants have to suffer only a few hours of minor discomfort crammed into Coach and can telephone their families to assure them of their safe arrival. In two generations, my family, like millions of others, discarded their language and traditions and history like so many moth-eaten coats and became Americans!

A lot was gained. My life has been easier than my parents' lives, and their lives have been far easier—not to mention safer—than those of their parents and grandparents. And a lot was lost, tradition and culture, the certainty of knowing who you are and where you belong. Maybe that's the way it has to be. But I wish I could feel more connected to the people who came before me. I'd like a deeper understanding of where I fit into the chain, a stronger sense of my place in the historical framework. I'd like that understanding for myself, and I'd very much like to pass it on my children and grandchildren. I hope, at least, that they begin asking questions before it is too late.

A CHILD OF THE FIFTIES

I remember walking the streets in the winter and looking in the windows and seeing that little gray screen. The entire nation was watching TV in the Fifties. No one was on the streets, or talking to their neighbor. We were the last people on our block to get a TV, we were the liberals, we weren't going to give in to that garbage, except that the kids spent every waking minute at our neighbors' watching TV. So my parents gave in. And we all fell into it.

—Lynn

I'd like to think of myself as a child of the Sixties, shaped by revolution and experimentation, but I have to admit that the culture and sensibilities of the Fifties exerted the most powerful influences on my life. Learning to dance to "Sh-Boom Sh-Boom," Friday nights at the Y, Buddy Holly, "White Port and Lemon Juice," poodle skirts and crinolines, matching cashmere sweater-and-skirt outfits in pink and blue, football games, glowering boys with duck-tail haircuts and packs of Camels tucked in the rolled sleeves of tight white T-shirts. Cruising El Camino Real in my friend Brooke's father's turquoise T-Bird, cherry cokes at one drive-in after another from San Bruno to Palo Alto and back again; where's the party? Weird kids on the fringes who dressed in black and read poetry to one another while the rest of us laughed and secretly wondered if we were missing out. In the background was another war, Korea at the other end of the world, stuffy old Eisenhower, Mamie with her silly cereal bowl haircut. McCarthy was spraying his poison at Commies behind the bushes. And we saw the first stirrings of the Civil Rights Movement that would, along with Vietnam, dominate our next decade, dogs and fire hoses turned on black children in the South, Brown vs. the Board of Education. We knew about such things because the country had discovered television.

> I was in third grade when we got our first TV. I used to watch Howdy Doody and Captain Fortune. On Saturday mornings we'd go to our friend's house to watch cowboy movies. Then, later, "I Remember Mama" with Maxwell House Coffee, "Father Knows Best," "Leave It to Beaver." I thought that was the world that we were supposed to be like. And my family just wasn't like that. For one thing, we weren't white.
>
> —Sachiko

Mine is the last generation to remember life before TV, and life before TV was radio: "The Shadow." "Burns and Allen." "Fibber McGee and Molly." I was eleven when we got our first TV. Until then, we'd sit around the living room after dinner and listen to the radio. My brother and I would do our homework or draw pictures. My father would read; my mother would knit. Some nights we'd play Monopoly or a game of cards. But that all changed with our first television. From 1951 on, we spent our evenings in front of The Box, and it was hard to do homework watching TV, hard to draw, impossible to read or play games. From that time on, all my information about the world, how I was supposed to behave, how I was supposed to look, how I was supposed to think, came—quite literally—from black and white TV, and black and white TV was "Ozzie and Harriet," "Our Miss Brooks," "I Love Lucy," "The Show of Shows," "The Donna Reed Show," "Leave It to Beaver": A white-picket-fence world inhabited by clean-cut white Christians who were not too bright, never swore, never farted, respected their elders, and always put work and responsibility ahead of pleasure. A world with lots of shoulds and shouldn'ts, lots of rights and wrongs. You should listen to your parents. You should go to church (Protestant). You should be proud to be American (White Anglo-Saxon Protestant). Do well in school. Never let your parents know you drink. It's okay to pet a little, but no sex! No sex!

You weren't supposed to have sex but you did. My older sister was the only girl in Topeka who was a virgin when she got married.
                                                            —Melva

One legacy of the Fifties is a truly schizophrenic attitude toward sex. I *never* remember talking about sex with my mother after the time she gave me, three weeks before my first period, a book that explained (sort of) the mysteries of menstruation. Even after decades of talking at great length about the most intimate details of our lives and psyches, my woman friends and I are still unable to talk easily about sex. So many taboos surrounded the subject when we were growing up. So many contradictions. We were expected to keep ourselves attractive, but not to engage in attracting behaviors. (When I was fourteen and weighed 98 pounds soaking wet, my mother made me wear a girdle. Nice girls in the Fifties wore bras and girdles and hose. You had to be careful not to let anything jiggle, or to show too much skin. The girdle was a metaphor for the way we were supposed to think about sex—hold it in, deny it, never show anyone that it's there.) We were expected to be desirable, but not to desire, to suppress any interest in sex until our wedding night when we were supposed instinctively to know how to please our husbands. Boys talked about sex all the time (at least we thought they did), joked about it, boasted—and lied—about their "conquests." But "good" girls talked about it only indirectly. Hinted, and suggested, and giggled. And lied. Only years later did I discover that most of my high school friends had lost their virginity well before graduation.

> I lost my virginity when I was sixteen, because I didn't know the difference between sex and love, and I was looking for love.
>
> —Maureen

> I was taught you never, ever get pregnant—unmarried, I mean. Even to this day I don't see how young girls get pregnant without being married, it was so ingrained in my head. You weren't supposed to have sex but you did, so the moral of the story was you damn well better not get pregnant. And if you did, you have to get married or have an abortion.
>
> —Melva

The good old double standard was in full swing during the Fifties. Boys were expected to do it and girls were expected not to do it, which of course raised the question of who the boys were expected to do it with. Everyone knew that the only time it was okay was if you were in love. One friend who lost her virginity well before high school graduation remembers sincerely believing that she was deeply in love with every boy she did it with. That, she told me, made it okay. But you had to be very, very careful (this was before the Pill that was to make the sexual revolution possible). So even though it might be okay to do it with someone you really loved, if you weren't careful and you got pregnant, you would have to get married. Or have an illegal abortion, which could kill you.

One of my most indelible memories from the early Fifties is of the afternoon that everyone—I mean *everyone*—learned from the local newspaper that my classmate's big sister had died from an amateur abortion. I can still see her picture on the front page, a yearbook photo, pretty smiling young face above the *de rigueur* white collar and pearls, side by side with a picture of the boy who had impregnated her and then given her a fatal combination of drugs from the pharmacy where he worked. His was not a yearbook photo. It was the stunned face of a teenaged boy who had made a terrible mistake. They had been desperate. They didn't want to get married. They didn't want to quit school and raise a child. They didn't want to confront their parents' anger and disappointment. I am sure they believed that their parents would be unforgiving, that no one would understand or help them, that they had done something forbidden and would be punished. Well, they certainly were punished.

Our parents must have been horrified, their worst fears made reality. They must have whispered about the tragedy for weeks, although I do not remember it being discussed; after all, talking about sex was almost as bad as doing it. Still, they found ways of making sure that we were warned not to Get Ourselves Pregnant Before Marriage.

What I remember most vividly, after the initial shock and excitement, was a sense that my friend's sister and her boyfriend were considered to be unquestionably at fault. It only came to me years later that there was something desperately wrong with a societal norm that would drive children to such a tragic act, with a society that offered them no acceptable alternatives.

And little has changed. Forty years later, despite a spreading but preventable sex-linked epidemic, so many teenagers are having unprotected sex that teenage pregnancy has become one of the country's most pressing problems. Do we respond by mounting a pull-out-all-the-stops effort to educate our children, to teach them about responsible sex, to show them how to protect themselves against a disease that will surely kill them? We do not. We continue to spout the same old Fifties line: No sex! No sex! What in the world do we think we are doing? Do we honestly think the kids are going to stop having sex? Did we?

> *When I grew up on the east side of Manhattan, propriety and convention were held to be the most important things. The way you behaved, the way you dressed, how you conducted yourself. Sliding through on mannerliness was more important than substance could ever be. Did you have on the right length white gloves? Well, I never did, and they were always dirty, because there was something else I was thinking about.*
>
> *—Susan*

The Fifties was chock-full of expectations that turned out to be difficult—or impossible—to meet. I realize that conventionality wasn't invented just for my teenage years; I've read Edith Wharton. But it was such a stifling time. The path seemed to be so clearly marked and so carefully manicured. You knew exactly where you were supposed to go and exactly how you were supposed to get there. You had few options: You followed that one right path ... or you had to forge new paths of your own. And that's what so many of us tried to do. At least, that's what we thought we were doing. It would take us years to discover that the "new" paths we created were not so different from the paths we'd been so determined not to follow. After all, you can take the girl out of the Fifties, but it's hard to take the Fifties out of the girl.

CHANGING THE WORLD

I believed we were going to change the world, and there was going to be peace. We all define ourselves very differently than we would have before. It become okay to have long gray hair and put a flower in it. A little weird, but okay. And I think it opened possibilities that can't ever be ignored. We'll never be people who never used drugs again, who didn't see the colors, the other levels of reality. We'll never be people who didn't experiment sexually again.

—Vivian

The Sixties changed the way I saw my world, and my place in that world. The Kennedys and King and Tricky Dick, Civil Rights and Vietnam, LSD and grass and peyote and sex and Woodstock. After the conformity and predictability and unblinking acceptance of authority of the Fifties, the shocking idea that millions of people could come together and say, "NO WAR!" and, in the end, be heard. The shocking idea that it was okay to be different and that there were different ways to live.

The most amazing external event was the Sixties. The change in the way you had to be. Maybe in the late Fifties, when I was practicing being a beatnik, dressing in black tights, having intense conversations about poetry and existentialism, it became possible to think for oneself. But that was still a pretty prescribed way of being. But the Sixties, with the emphasis on becoming an individual with freedom to be who you are, being different from society as a whole. Rebelling against society, against the established institutions, from the music, to the dancing, to drugs, looking at politics differently, it was okay to be liberal, okay not to have children, okay not to get married. Okay to have sex. It seemed like everything that had not been okay but had always seemed okay to me suddenly was okay. It seemed to me that there was hope there, a hope there had never been before, that we could really change things.

—Vivian

The feeling I had always had about not fitting in, about wanting something different than I was supposed to want—suddenly everyone I knew felt that way. Not only felt, but acted on. The sense that you were supposed to look a certain way, dress a certain way, behave in a certain way, that there was this grownup book and *this* is what happens: All that was burst open. For the first time in my life it was okay to have curly hair and ask "Why" all the time. We certainly did ask: "*Why* should we do that? *What* does all this have to do with anything?" And it was no longer acceptable to answer, "Because that's the way it is." It became possible to say, "No, that's not the way I want to do it; I want to try this way." That felt wonderful to me.

The shift from the Fifties to the Sixties was "heady" for me, the vision of society, that there were alternatives, there wasn't just the Donna Reed show, the rigidity of the nuclear family, and the vaguely Christian background that dominated everything, some polite, nice, clean thing, and the nice clean mother who stayed home and looked after everything and the daddy who provided money but otherwise was a little bit ridiculous. That was so narrow-minded

*and so rigid. We discovered there was a whole other world,
with many ways of living and thinking.*

—Lynn

Although the Sixties was completely unlike anything I had foreseen for myself, I was ready. More than ready. I said, "Oh, yeah, that's the way it's supposed to be, that's *right.*" I joyously embraced what was happening as a lifeline, joined my friends in their head-long rush to discard the beliefs and values and conventions they had brought to San Francisco from Alabama and Michigan and Nebraska and New Jersey and Kansas. We *had* to discard them. We couldn't have explained why. We just knew.

Even today, when they show clips from the Fifties TV comedies, I can feel just how stultifying it was. I used to pace the streets at night looking for something different. I read books all the time, devoured them. I felt totally different from anybody I knew until I was in college and met a few mavericks. There was one girl on our block who started to question the Catholic faith that she had grown up in, and we used to go ice skating and try to have philosophical debates amid all the jocks and cheerleaders who were skating by. But there was so little questioning, and so few alternatives.

—Lynn

First of all, it gave you choices. Lifestyle choices. Trivial choices, hairstyles and hemlines, and country vs. city. It said, no barriers, period. Political choices.

—Leslie

So many of us needed to ask questions and find new ways of looking at the world, new ways of living. But it was such a complicated decade, with many contradictions and many abrupt changes.

In the early Sixties it was telephone bars, "Hello cutie at Table 16," sorority parties, and Jackie Kennedy hairdos, and in a flash it became granny dresses and tie-dyed T-shirts and taking off our clothes in the park and blocking busloads of draftees at the Oakland Army terminal and closing down the colleges. Everything seemed to change within a couple of years: First it was folk music in coffeehouses and people in black smoking funny cigarettes, and then it was the Beatles, Dylan, Joan Baez ... music as consciousness raising. From 1966 on, a fog of dope and protest marches, Wavy Gravy and the Black Panthers, the Grateful Dead and Ken Kesey, and Revolution! Except that it wasn't, not really. I'm always surprised to find that many people my age knew "my" Sixties only on TV, just as I'm surprised to learn that a commune still survives outside of Bloomington, Indiana.

> I went to college in the Sixties. Washington University in Topeka, Kansas. I was aware of what was happening in San Francisco, but what I was the most aware of was Martin Luther King Jr. We were in sit-ins, things like that. The Civil Rights Movement was much more meaningful to us. Linda Brown, Brown vs. the Board of Education, was someone I went to school with. We knew this other stuff was going on, the Beatles, Elvis Presley, but we lived in a very different world. We didn't care. It didn't affect us. Martin Luther King Jr. marching did affect me. You sort of felt, like with Woodstock, they just have to think up something to protest. It was okay, but it wasn't my thing. It was a white-middle-class-kids' movement. It wasn't my experience.
>
> —Melva

We do tend to think of our experience as the *only* experience, and our perspectives as the *only* perspectives. Those of us who lived in the Haight, danced in Golden Gate Park, fought for People's Park in Berkeley, joined anti-war demonstrations, and camped out at Woodstock thought of that time as unique, momentous. "The biggest change in the history of the world." "We changed the world forever," one friend said, quite seriously, quite sincerely. How arrogant we are. Do we think that World War II didn't change the world? World War I? The Depression? The Suffragettes? The Russian Revolution? The Industrial Revolution? The American Revolution? The Revolution in China? Napoleon? Jesus? The Buddha? Muhammad? Gandhi? The inventions of the wheel and the printing press? A mere quarter of a century later many of the ripples we thought were tidal waves have disappeared without a trace. Even Jane Fonda sold out, married a captain of industry and apologized (apologized!) for her actions protesting the war. Sure, many of us were changed by our experiences, but it certainly wasn't "the biggest change in the history of the world." And we sometimes forget that certain events, certain changes, were not so wonderful. For one thing, we lost our heroes.

> *The single event I remember most was when Kennedy was shot. I don't know whether it was pivotal, but it was really the end of Camelot.*
> *—Anita*

> *I think the most important events for me were the serial events of the assassination of both of the Kennedys and Martin Luther King Jr. What they represented to me was that I was no longer safe. That the world had shattered. And so had my ideals. Along came Lyndon Baines Johnson, who I thought was just … scum city. Gone was my wonderful sense of we could change, we could make a differ-*

ence. And I think at that point I turned in, as opposed to
out, away from the possibility of effecting change.

—Susan

Twenty-five years after the Summer of Love, I find myself on
Haight Street. It's dirty. Glassy-eyed children huddle in doorways
and hunker down in clumps on the sidewalks. Pornographic newspapers sit openly in street-corner racks. Homeless women push
their children down the street in shopping carts. Tour buses make
their way through the traffic, carrying travelers from Paris and
London and Tokyo and Lincoln, Nebraska, through San Francisco's
version of a Disneyland exhibit. I can still feel a certain energy,
but the innocence is gone. And I remember that Charlie Manson
once lived only two blocks up the hill, and I see that there were
only two or three years of innocence, of trust, of love your brother
(and sister), before the whole thing began to come apart.

I got discouraged towards the end of the Sixties when
that whole thing got exploited and fell in upon itself—
drug dealing, mysticism that was out of touch with day-
to-day realities. The people who were most interesting
were the ones who could balance idealism and getting
the dishes done. And the hippie dream ended, and the
people who had any dream left went off to the Oregon
forest to raise goats. Everyone fled. Some people would
say it was like a pine cone bursting and seeds scattering.
That's debatable.

—Leslie

We were kids, after all. And we were having such a good
time. In retrospect—that point of view where everything becomes
clear—it's not surprising what happened next, that the mellow,
loving Sixties changed into the more brittle Seventies and the

greedy Eighties. "Do your own thing, be happy." "I am I and you are you, and if by chance we find each other, it's beautiful." Thanks, Fritz Perls, but is that the way it's supposed to work? It's fine to be responsible *to* yourself, if you are also responsible *for* yourself. *And for one another.*

Once "do your own thing" became more important than "love your brother (and sister)," the me-me generation was inevitable. Werner Erhard's EST—your problem is not my problem. Whoever has the most toys wins. Michael Milken. Donald Trump as hero.

> *I think we were selfish brats. And it led directly to the me-me generation. I never thought the supposed altruism of the Sixties was very altruistic. At the beginning it was, with the Civil Rights Movement. But by the time the flower children came along, it was a very large party.*
>
> *—Margo*

So what did it all mean, "The Sixties"? Is Margo right? Was it only a big party, or did we create any meaningful long-lasting change? Well, it was a lot of fun. We also did create change, in important ways. For example: It's no longer a crime to be different. I saw a young girl the other day with shaved head, pasty white face, and something glittery in her upper lip, and all I thought was, "Hm, that's somebody's baby girl." I didn't particularly like the way she looked, but I felt no need to condemn her. (That's easier to say when it's not one of your kids.) We tolerate a wider variety of lifestyles. My parents didn't even mention the M-word when my daughter announced she was moving in with her boyfriend, and one friend whose Midwestern mother insisted that she wear white gloves to go shopping talks openly about her daughter's lesbian relationships. We at least pay lip service to the concept that it's wrong to discriminate against people because of their race, ethnicity, gender, or physical disability. It's not that we no longer discriminate; it's that we don't do it as openly as we used to, and we at least promote the idea that it's wrong. Sex is no longer a dirty word, although bared female breasts still occasion the sort of outrage that should be reserved for the sight of an AK 47. We seem more ready to expect and accept change. We even know we can make change happen, if we're willing to work at it. And we know that it's possible to question authority—although these days we seldom seem to bother.

> *I think of the Sixties as a lot of idealism, as hope. I think we carry hope, a feeling that there must be some solution to the problem. I think younger people have a more difficult time with that.*
>
> —*Sachiko*

I miss the Sixties, the way I miss my youth. But it's more than that. As Americans become more polarized on issues ranging from abortion to affirmative action to immigration, I find myself yearning for a new Sixties, a new upsurge in energy, focus, and hope. I yearn for that sense of community we seemed to have, that sense of people banding together and stirring things up to make change happen. In the midst of the party, an entire generation—two generations and a smattering of enlightened "elders"—fought together for changes in unfair and unjust government policies ... and won. What have we done since? During the Desert Storm debacle, I wanted desperately to believe that all us grownup hippies and wannabe hippies who shouted, "Make Love Not War," would return to the streets and refuse to allow our children to go to war over oil in the Middle East, refuse to allow the death and mutilation of thousands of young people to prop up yet another friendly tyranny. We did make a few small noises, but we were lucky: It was over before our children were called, before we were too clearly challenged. We did not make much protest when other people's children were sent off to the battlefield.

What's going on? Are we too old now, too settled, too comfortable, too apathetic, to fight together against genocide in the Baltics, against poverty and homelessness and toxic waste and bigotry at home, against the destruction of the rain forests, against the greed and corruption that's destroying our economy? Can't we still find the energy and will to demand a change of political focus? What *did* we teach our children? And where the hell are the kids when you need them?

AN IMPERFECT VESSEL

NO MORE SHORT SHORTS

And then I am 47 ... and my infirmities will of course increase. To begin with, my eyes. Last year, I think, I could read without spectacles ... gradually I found I needed spectacles in bed; and now I can't read a line (unless held at a very odd angle) without them ... I can hear, I think, perfectly; I think I could walk as well as ever. But then will there not be the change of life? (Virginia Woolf, A Writer's Diary)

I am continually amazed at how old young has become ... Now all of a sudden, I'm older than my parents were when I thought they were old. (Lois Wyse, Funny, You Don't Look Like a Grandmother)

I have an indelible memory of adolescence, when I was obsessed beyond reason with my changing body. When I had my first period, at age eleven, the thick cotton pad between my legs was the size of a bed pillow; surely everyone could see. At recess, my friends and I crowded around the mirror in the girls' room, layering Clearasil on our faces like greasepaint. I secretly stuffed my A-cups with Kleenex as I waited anxiously for my minuscule breasts to swell so they would drive boys mad with desire. (I was to be sadly disappointed.) I longed for thinner thighs, straighter hair, longer eyelashes, a straighter nose, and a smaller waist the way I would later in life long for a shiny new car or a month in Paris.

I guess the main thing to me is the clear realization of not being young anymore. There's a part in me that feels very young. And I go into stores and I look at clothes and I think, those are for women, for old people, grownup women, they're too old for me. I never look at those. And now I'm starting to think, "But who are they for if not for me?"

—Vivian

Around forty for me was, okay, I'm not a teenager, I can't wear pigtails any more. It's very hard for me still; I go into Loehmann's and I can't buy short shorts. I want to be able to do everything. It's foolish, however, not to acknowledge that you can't. You can push the line, but just barely. It's like being a hippie in the Nineties. You're going to look stupid.

—Leslie

My son, a fan of the Grateful Dead, pays hard-earned money to watch middle-aged men cavort on stage. On the freeways I see men with bushy gray hair and bifocals and middle-aged women with long straight hair and granny glasses and flabby upper arms driving battered vans sporting Grateful Dead stickers. I think, "These are people out of time. That's not me. I've kept up." Well … I think I keep up. But sometimes I don't recognize the line I'm not supposed to cross. I no longer know what's appropriate. It becomes important to reconcile, or at least accept, the basic conflicts—perceptions and misperceptions, image and reality.

I'm bothered by the slacking of my body, and even though I exercise, everything's sagging and sinking and falling and flabbing, and that's disheartening.

—Judy

It's come back, that adolescent obsession with body. My face has begun to deteriorate. My hair has been thinning and fading for several years, and now it's turning gray. My eyelids sag. My frown lines grow deeper. Losing weight does not reduce the telltale bulge of my belly. My upper arms are too fleshy for sleeveless shirts.

And the tradeoff? I grow wiser. I become more able to see what will happen, to see farther along the continuum into the past and into the future from a single event. I begin to know what matters.

Is that enough?

In our culture it is difficult to be old, and still live with younger fellowmen … (M. F. K. Fisher, *Sister Age*)

My cousin and I examine each other's faces. We have the same folds that droop over our eyelids, the same deep pouches under our eyes, the same jowls that start just below our mouths. We think the same thought: "Facelift."

From the outward appearance I will be thought of as an older person, middle-aged. Never matronly—I won't allow that. So I'm going to do everything in my power not to let that happen. When I can afford it, I am going to get a facelift. To me, anything anybody does to help themselves feel better, and to help their self-esteem, is a plus, and for me, that's a facelift. I figure I'm probably good for one in my lifetime. And around fifty will be the perfect time to do it. I'll still be physically healthy enough to enjoy it.

—Judy

My friends are divided on the issue of surgery and other medical techniques to ward off the outward signs of aging. Certainly movie stars and models and other women whose beauty is their meal ticket have no such compunctions. But my cousin and I are not movie stars or models. We're just ordinary women. The thing is, unless you're Michelle Pfeiffer, or Cher, or Joan Collins, or Jane Fonda, or Elizabeth Taylor, beauty *is* youth. Beauty is twenty, twenty-two. This is not about beauty. It's about—freshness. It's about—making it more comfortable for young people to be with us, it's about—fitting in. So when my hairdresser offered a free color treatment, to "put the life back into my hair," I said, "Okay." I was curious. Would more youthful hair change my life? Would my friends notice that I looked better, not sure why, and ask whether I'd lost weight? Would men once again approach me in the grocery store to ask my advice on choosing tomatoes?

I got the color, and I was peeved that no one, not even my husband, noticed. Nevertheless, I liked the way my hair once again picked up the light. It didn't make me younger. But it made me happier with the image in my mirror. So I'll probably do what my hairdresser hoped I'd do, shell out an extra fifty dollars every eight weeks or so to keep the color.

> *I have gray hair, and all my friends said I should dye my hair, and I never wanted to. But I did. I dyed my hair. I'm not into tummy tucks, and that sort of thing. I'm not that type of person.*
>
> *—Maureen*

The consensus among my friends seems to be that it's okay to:
> dye your hair (everyone does)
> reshape your body through exercise (thanks, Jane Fonda)
> spend money on chemicals and cosmetics such as anti-
>   aging creams and Retin-A
> have breast implants if you have a mastectomy

Not okay to:

> have tummy tucks, facelifts, and other plastic surgery
>
> have liposuction
>
> get collagen injections
>
> have breast implants for cosmetic reasons only

What an amazing discussion! What would my grandmother, who struggled to keep food on the table during the Depression, make of this debate? Or her mother, who I picture in thick cloth coat and babushka on the deck of the ship that brought her from Russian pogroms to the land of liberty where she was free to work eighteen hours a day to support her fatherless children? These are truly issues of the Nineties. We are the first generation to have available safe, inexpensive methods of preserving a youthful appearance. Because we have the means, we must decide: Is preserving a youthful appearance a worthwhile goal?

So where do I stand? I'm certainly comfortable using creams to keep my skin from drying out, exercising to keep my body fit, adding color to my fading hair. If a cheap, painless procedure comes on the market to tighten up my sagging chinline or drooping eyelids—well, maybe. But I cannot see myself resorting to cutting or injections, if for no other reason than I am never willing to tolerate pain.

And yet ... long, long ago, in the name of beauty, I deliberately and with forethought paid out an entire summer's earnings so a plastic surgeon could break and reshape my nose, and I never regretted the decision. So as I take my position in the anti-cutting, anti-injecting camp, I won't judge my cousin and friends who opt for, to me, radical measures to be perceived as younger than they are. Every woman has to decide for herself what kind of body image she needs, and what she is willing to do to achieve it.

And ... I reserve the right to change my mind.

By forty-five I had to accept either that I had a horrible secret disease or that as you get older you have diminished energy. I can no longer party all night, play tennis in the morning, and still have energy left over for other things. I've never thought of myself as an energetic person, but now that I'm losing what little I have, I really miss it.

—*Lynn*

The external changes are only, as they say, the tip of the iceberg. The important changes are less obvious to the observer but more worrisome to me.

Of course, turning fifty is just a day; it doesn't mean anything. But a few years ago, I began noticing that I didn't have quite the energy, quite the strength I had before. It was almost funny at first. Look at this. Could this be because of age, or could it be because I'm not feeling very well? It became clear to me that I have less physical strength and energy than I had before, at times, not always. And that was a shock. I guess the main thing to me is the clear realization of not being young anymore.

—*Vivian*

We know how to take care of ourselves. We eat low-fat foods. We jog. We swim. We work out at the gym. Unlike our parents, we seldom drink hard liquor, although we enjoy good wine with dinner. We stopped smoking years ago. We've found ways to reduce our stress—yoga classes, massages, long walks, long talks, a change of scene. We've stopped trying to be all things to all people. We no longer think of ourselves as superwoman.

Even so, the effects of aging are impossible to deny. I can exhaust myself by doing an ordinary day's work or playing tennis on a hot afternoon. And I get tired differently now. My throat gets dry. My eyes water. My shoulders ache. My thinking slows. I feel heavy, dull, worn out. It's not the kind of tired I felt when I was twenty-five and could spend most of a night partying, sleep for three hours and go off to work. Or when I was thirty-five and a quick nap would set me up for the evening. Now I feel exhausted, stunned, and I don't bounce back. I don't get a second wind. I am fit only to crawl into bed at ten o'clock while other (younger) people are out there having fun.

> I've noticed that my memory is not as good as it used to be. When I'm tired, or under stress, I'll transpose words, or say something I don't mean, insert another word. And people will catch me. It's rather embarrassing, especially when I'm on the bench. It's like a lapse of consciousness. It may be a function of aging.
> —Anita

I drift off in the middle of a conversation, in the middle of a class, wake up to a room full of confused faces, and I realize I haven't been making sense. Maybe it is a function of aging. Maybe it's overwork, preoccupation, boredom. Or maybe it's the first stage of Alzheimer's; I feel a twinge of panic.

From my journal:

> Feeling old this weekend, exhausted by an afternoon of tennis in the hot sun, a day on the Bay. The word "stunned" has come up twice since Friday, first in a Joseph Hansen mystery where the aging detective admits he is "stunned" by martinis in his dotage, again last night at Margaret's when Sherril confided that she felt "stunned" by her impending fiftieth birthday. I, too, feel stunned. My cheeks burn. My head swims, although it is only 9:30 in the morning and I slept (nearly) the whole night through. Is this

what really separates youth from age? Will I need forever more to consider my shallow storehouse of strength before embarking on an adventure? I know, I know. This is a broken record. "Strength." "Energy." "Stamina." It's getting boring. But I feel so stunned by the sense that life as I've known it has been transformed, that I have been transformed. I am a moth emerging from the cocoon to find myself a different sort of being. Only—I have no wings.

Buried in last week's newspaper was mention of an experimental hormone replacement therapy that appears to increase energy and make older people feel younger than their years. What an exciting prospect, to feel again the way I felt at thirty-five, with deep stores of energy and clarity of thought (or what I remember as clarity of thought). Imagine the power of an old person whose mind is crystal clear and who doesn't get tired! I wouldn't mind. (Still, my conscience prods: I hope that the people who fund this research understand that a long-shot "cure" for the symptoms of old age must take a back seat to far more pressing issues, not the least of which is finding a cure for AIDS. Otherwise, an old-age cure won't matter one whit.)

But getting old *is* getting tired, and if relief is to come from medical science, I suspect it will come for the baby boomers, not for me. I must assume that my energy will continue to diminish. That's a fact. There's no use denying it, or worrying about it, or waiting anxiously for a miracle cure. Instead, I will try to focus. I will choose carefully the way I spend this precious but limited resource. I will decide what's important to me and what's not, discriminate among what I must do, what I want to do, and what I do only out of habit. I will seek activities that refresh and energize me. I will slow myself down. I will use all my senses.

NOT THE BABY BOOMERS

BOOMERS REDEFINE THE NEW AGE OF OLD AGE
(Headline in the *San Francisco Chronicle*, September 22, 1991)

Is there really more talk about aging? Or do I notice the talk because I *am* aging, the way you notice ads for new cars when your brakes get soft? I think it's real. By the early 1990s, when I was moving into my sixth decade, the subject was definitely starting to get more attention. In the *Harvard Business Review*: an article on "The Aging Workforce"; in *Vanity Fair*: Gail Sheehy on menopause, "The Last Taboo"; on the bookshelf: Germaine Greer's *The Change: Women, Aging and the Menopause*; on National Public Radio: a seventy-year-old woman who saw life as a constant learning experience and said she only started to live at age forty-two; and in my local newsrag, the *San Francisco Chronicle*: historian Page Smith's weekly column, "Coming of Age." For a while, it seemed that every week brought yet another article or news feature on some aspect of aging: "Coming of Age" (*Savvy*), "Aging Baby Boomers Tempt Real Estate Investors" (*Chronicle*), "New Moms at Fortysomething" (*Chronicle*), "20 Good Things That Happen When You Grow Older" (*McCall's*), "Fiftysome-thing" (*Chronicle*), "The Myth of Middle Age" (*Chronicle*), "GAME PLAN FOR FITNESS AFTER 40" (*Chronicle*).

The numbers alone are staggering . . . . In 1988, 76 million people were 45 or older—a full 31 percent of the population, a percentage that is increasing rapidly . . . [what we now see] is a reinterpretation of the definition of aging

.... Cher, in 1991, is 45 ... at 40-plus, the Rolling Stones and the Grateful Dead are still rocking ... 42 percent of the runners who finished the 1989 New York Marathon were over 40 ... (Faith Popcorn, "The Popcorn Report," *San Francisco Chronicle*, September 22, 1991)

It's not *my* generation that's attracting the attention. It's the so-called baby boomers, those 77 million children born between 1946 and 1964. The baby boomers are my generation's younger sisters and brothers. From our point of view, they're still kids. They're only starting to lose their waistlines, only beginning to squint at small print. It's wonderful that they've finally settled down, adopted kinder, gentler lifestyles, taken out mortgages, had kids of their own, and learned to cook. But our waistlines are gone for good. We've already changed our bifocal prescriptions several times. Our babies are grown and gone; we're getting ready to sell the family homestead and move to a maintenance-free condo somewhere warm. The baby boomers are juggling like crazy, but we're changing direction again, and we're starting to slow down.

The people studying and writing about the aging baby boomers send a clear message: These people are growing older *differently. They* aren't going to succumb easily to the ravages of age. *They* are going to look terrific, feel terrific, and keep on playing ... forever.

I was at my gym the other day, in the changing room, and there was a woman next to me who had to be in her sixties. I couldn't stop sneaking looks at her body, everything sagging. It was disgusting. I thought, "How can she stand it?"

—Overheard remark

The woman who said that appeared to be in her mid- to late

thirties and probably sees forty coming up fast. Forty frightens her. Fifty is "elderly." I've got news for you, kid. If a sagging body is your greatest fear, you might as well give up now. Because no matter how carefully you eat, how hard you exercise, how many facelifts and tummy tucks and collagen injections you get, you're *still* going to get old. Your breasts will droop. Your hair will lose its pigmentation. Your skin will dry and become less elastic and you will get wrinkles. You will almost certainly need reading glasses or bifocals. It will become a constant struggle to keep your size 6 figure. You'll tire more easily and bounce back less quickly. Like everyone else, you *will* slow down, and one day you will die.

Maybe it's the difference in ages. Maybe you actually have to *experience* the changes in your body before you fully understand what getting older really means. Only the oldest of the baby boomers (such as my little brother, who turned fifty a few months ago), and of course, Hillary, Bill, Al, and Tipper) are close to being there. Not only are they saying, "We want to grow older *differently*," they seem to be saying, "We are not *really* going to get old. We're going to beat this thing. We're going to be young forever."

One mourns one's young face sometimes. I now use a night cream for the first time in my life. At the same time ... I feel that my face is better now ... That is because I am a far more complete and richer person than I was at twenty-five, when ambition and personal conflicts were paramount, and there was a surface of sophistication that was not true of the person inside. Now I wear the inside person outside and am more comfortable with my self. (May Sarton, At Seventy: A Journal)

At fifty-five, my body has made it clear that I'm no longer young. Last year I developed something called "frozen shoulder," which my acupuncturist tells me is known in China as "fifties shoulder." Whatever it's called, I couldn't reach with my left arm or turn over in bed for months. My hips ache when I sit in one position too long. What's left of my hair is turning gray. I know that this physical deterioration will continue, and that one day I will be old. I don't like the idea, but it seems pointless to deny reality, which is what I suspect the baby boomers are still trying to do. Well, it's not denial I'm after, it's acceptance. I want to accept the fact that I'm getting old, and I want to go through the process differently from the women who preceded me, just as I always wanted to live my life somewhat differently than they lived theirs. I have some ideas about what "differently" means: Keeping myself healthy and strong, remaining involved in meaningful activities, taking risks, continuing to learn, living completely in the moment as often as I can. What feels important to me now is to accept what I do not like but cannot change about aging and free myself to embrace the gifts.

My generation, born as the world was launching itself into World War II, spent much of our lives forging paths for the baby boomers. Now we're doing it again by exploring different ways of getting old, experimenting with different lifestyles and alternative living environments, starting new careers in midlife, challenging the taboos on sexuality for older women. We have a few role models among our parents' generation (after all, they were the people who created the concept of "active retirement"), but we're still scrabbling in the dark. Still, our efforts to redefine old age might open up possibilities for the boomers—as soon as they wake up and read the writing on the wall.

THE CHANGE

When I thought I was getting menopausal, that was scary. I was feeling at the end of my female—I don't even like the word menopause. I asked my gynecologist, "Should I take hormones?" And he said, "You have to take them for fifteen years." And I said, "Then what happens? Do you get hot flashes again?" And he said, "Don't worry about it. In the old days, you would be dead." It feels as if there is some real biological thing, triggering mortality.

—Leslie

One day, tears in the middle of tennis. The next morning, outlook sunny.

"Menopause," Jeffery says.

"Of course not," I say. "Don't even say that word to me," I snap.

She must have gone through menopause. She looked, you know, old.

—An overheard remark

Menopause. Everyone knows what *that* means. It's The Change that Heralds the Slide into Old Age. I've avoided discussing it. I try not to think about it. I can color my hair all I want, maybe even give in and get a tummy tuck, but I can't deny that menopause means getting old. Menopause means being transferred, against my will, into new category: "Women Who Are Past the Change," sexless women who live on the fringe of society, who have outlived their usefulness, who are fragile, who must be taken care of. Women who are ignored. Lonely, bored, tired, ugly, purposeless, *old* women.

On the other hand, maybe I haven't been getting enough sleep.

> *One reason for the mystery surrounding menopause is that human females today are monkeying with evolution. Most higher primates do not live long enough ... to have a menopause ... [they] just go on breeding until they roll over and die.* (Gail Sheehy, "The Last Taboo," *Vanity Fair*, September 1991)

> *The average woman in the U.S. and Canada can expect to live almost thirty years past menopause—a span of years that she wants to make as healthy and productive as possible.* (*University of California at Berkeley Wellness Letter*, October 1995)

I keep reminding myself that menopause is different now. It used to be that women could expect to die not long after their menses stopped, not because they'd outlived their usefulness, but because they had reached the end of a relatively short lifespan. They didn't have the advantages of the good nutrition, modern medicine, and easier lives that have given us another lifetime to live after our children have left. So just as it's no longer necessary to envision middle-aged women in print dresses and stout shoes, it's no longer necessary to hold onto an outdated image of menopause as the end of life. It's no longer necessary to talk about it in whispers, either. Last week's newspaper carried the headline, "View of Menopause as Disaster Fades Away," above a story about the North American Menopause Society, which "gathered in San Francisco to reject the idea that menopause is a time of debilitation and disease." (*San Francisco Examiner*, September 24, 1995)

Even in this Brave New World, however, menopause is still a physical and psychological passage for middle-aged women, and the physical part at least requires some difficult decisions. I listen as Vivian talks in hushed tones, seeking advice from our mutual friend Diane.

"I no longer want to ward off menopause with estrogen," Vivian says, "but I can't decide." Stop the drug, risk hot flashes and sleepless nights, uncomfortable but bearable, certainly. Risk osteoporosis and heart disease, not bearable, certainly. Take the drug, risk breast cancer. Also not bearable. "How can I put that stuff in my body every day while I'm meditating in India?" Vivian leans forward, shoulders hunched, seeking a solution. "Women never used to face this question. They went through menopause naturally. They survived."

"They had no choice," Diane responds. "I take antihistamines every day. My body wants to sneeze all the time. I do better when I take the drugs."

"I don't know what to do. It feels so wrong."

This conversation is of intense interest to me. My periods now come erratically, nothing for three months, then every two weeks for who knows how long. I wake in the night, my nightshirt and sheets soaking wet. I break into a sweat during meetings with clients, frantically open my collar and roll up my sleeves and pray that drops of sweat don't start rolling down my cheeks. I know I need information, but I forget to buy the books; I forget to raise the subject with my doctor. One night at dinner my friend Margaret confides that, bothered by incessant hot flashes and the sense that she was losing focus, she has begun estrogen replacement therapy, but I listen with scant attention. I still don't understand the difference between "ERT" and "HRT" (hormone replacement therapy). Only recently did I finally ask my mother about her own menopause, was it early or late, difficult or easy? Clearly, I do not feel an overwhelming desire to learn more about this thing happening to my body that only proves I'm getting old.

> *I have felt physical changes. I have PMS real bad. It's very disorienting. I'll be driving and I can't remember where I'm going. That part of aging has been very difficult. Very frightening. I thought I had Alzheimer's. But it's all part of menopause.*
>
> —Maureen

I am so easily distracted. Instead of concentrating on what's happening to my body, I become preoccupied with the question: Take the drug, don't take the drug. Modern medicine allows us so many choices. My mind wanders to all the questions we are able to ask today that could not have been asked, even conceived of, during the greater part of my lifetime. The question of whether to take a drug that will ease my transition into old age occupies a minor place on the importance scale when I consider other questions that are far more significant: Should doctors use machines to keep brain-dead children alive? Should infertile couples rent other women's bodies as surrogate wombs? Should people be allowed to sell their livers? Should we use our increasing knowledge about human genes to "design" children so they will not be born with inherited diseases? Today's science now gives us science-fiction options, and those options force us to answer gut-wrenching questions. I wonder what's more difficult, making the decisions posed by all those options—or living without them? It's a meaningless question; once the possibility is there, we can only choose to accept or reject it. We cannot pretend it doesn't exist. Still, I worry about crossing lines. I believe that out there somewhere are lines we *must not* cross.

Enough distraction. Those profound observations haven't done a thing to help me decide what to do about my own menopause. I need to do the reading. I need to decide whether to take the drugs or let nature have its way with me. One of these days, I will become motivated by discomfort or fear to take some action. But not today. Today, I have other, more pleasing things to do—take a walk, write a story, have lunch with a friend, clean out my closet ... . I'll think about menopause tomorrow.

AN OBJECT OF DESIRE

Whereas man grows old gradually, woman is suddenly deprived of her femininity; she is still relatively young when she loses the erotic attractiveness and the fertility which, in the view of society and in her own, provide the justification of her existence and her opportunity for happiness. With no future, she still has about one half of her adult life to live. (Simone de Beauvoir, The Second Sex)

Everyone knows that middle-aged women are not sexy. Not even interested in sex. Mom and Dad might give each other big warm hugs right there in the living room, but you don't think they still do it? (Giggle) After all, women don't do it after a certain age, at least they don't enjoy it, well, women never did enjoy it much anyway, what a relief finally to be able to give it up. Men are different. They have these drives. You expect men to keep doing it, and if they no longer find their wives attractive, if their wives refuse, you expect a man to find a younger woman to do it with. You see it in the movies. Male stars like Sean Connery and Robert Redford are routinely paired with women half their age (Michelle Pfeiffer, Demi Moore), but you sure don't see Jane Fonda or Shirley Maclaine in bed with Brad Pitt or Tom Cruise. "Northern Exposure" fans don't seem to find it odd that the teenage Shelly lusts after sixty-something Hollis, but they'd respond with guffaws if crusty old Marge went after thirty-something Chris. Sex and older men is part of the fabric of life. Sex and older women is a bad joke.

Sam said something to me the other night, and he encapsulated the compliment with, "For a fifty-year-old woman … " My response was to look around and see who he was talking about because it couldn't possibly be me.

—Susan

The public doesn't want to see an old puss giving the news. (Joan Rivers on "Fresh Air," November 8, 1991)

Making it into middle age means confronting all the myths and realities that surround sex for women. Most of us have spent our adult lives trying to attract or fend off male attention; suddenly it's become difficult to do the former and rarely necessary to do the latter. Lest we forget ourselves, the media reminds us, day after day, that sexiness for women equates with youth. From my seat near the magazine racks in a cafe, I can't help but notice that two of every three magazine covers are graced by a beautiful young woman exhibiting luscious young breasts, flawless skin, shiny hair, and long smooth legs. One morning I watched my husband of twenty-seven years, a man who is profoundly disinterested in fashion, leaf through an entire Sunday fashion supplement while sipping his morning coffee. When I saw the cover, I understood: His interest had been piqued by a blond bombshell, waist cinched tightly to throw her hips into relief, breasts ballooning out of a Wonderbra, shiny red lips pouting, shadowed eyes teasing—titillation with the morning toast. You'd have to be Helen Keller to miss the sexual images used to sell everything from automobiles to deodorant. Only someone who is blind and deaf could fail to notice that for women, every single one of those sexual images is young.

Why do you think we start trying to lose weight when we turn fifty? Why do we talk about diet all the time? Retin-A and facelifts and stuff. Because we recognize in some way the thing we fear most about turning fifty is that sexuality goes.

—Susan

I always look at movie stars in my age group. Mary Tyler Moore. Her face looks like a truck has run over it, but she's skinny. Her husband is over ten years younger than she is. And I thought, "Is that ridiculous or what?"

—Melva

I think most women enjoy the attention they receive from men, even if they're settled into a satisfactory long-term relationship. It's fun to engage in mild flirtations with attractive men in the grocery store or the post office, to carry a secret crush and speculate on the possibility of reciprocation. It's disappointing when instead of flirting, a man turns away when he registers my age, painful to realize that letting my "crush" know how I feel would probably evoke embarrassment, not reciprocated interest. As the mother of a daughter, I first noticed the signs when I was in my middle forties (and looked several years younger); once Jennifer reached her mid-teens, men we encountered, no matter what their ages, were far more interested in her than in me.

Our standards of physical and sexual attractiveness are still inexorably youth-oriented. Think of the advertisements for perfumes, lingerie, bathing suits—anything that entails a measure of nudity and eroticism ... the models are young or youthful-looking women. The implication is that to be sexy you must be young. (Herant Katchadourian, *Midlife in Perspective*)

Even ... where things are equal (and they seldom are),
the older woman cannot cruise the sex scene the way
that a man of the same age can. She is simply not per-
ceived as a sexual entity, unless she makes an unsubtle
display of herself ... which is a turn-off to all but the least
desirable partners. She then exposes herself in a buyers'
market, and the results to her physical and mental health
... can be ruinous. (Germaine Greer, *The Change*)

Now in my mid-fifties, I find that I am no longer "woman,"
but "middle-aged woman." There's a chilling definition of what
that means in Milan Kundera's book, *Immortality*. The male narrator describes an encounter between a middle-aged woman and
a young lifeguard on a cruise ship. The woman, in her fifties or
early sixties, had been observed flirting with the lifeguard at the
swimming pool. The narrator was fascinated, saddened, and dis-
gusted by this woman who still thought of herself as a *woman*,
who still thought of herself as sexually attractive, failing to understand that the changes in her body made her ugly, not an object of
desire, but an object of pity. I remember thinking as I read, "You
arrogant condescending son-of-a-bitch." And I felt sad. I felt a
sense of loss, a certain pity for my aging self, for this middle-aged
me who would invite ridicule if she were to forget herself momen-
tarily and flirt with an attractive man, if she were to let herself
believe that the sexuality she still felt on the inside conveyed itself on the outside the way it did when she was young.

A fifty-year-old man seen in the company of a twenty-
five-year-old wife or lover generates a very different kind
of social reaction than a fifty-year-old woman with a
twenty-five-year-old husband or lover ... These traditional
patterns are now changing ... but the shift to parity in

this respect is still far from being complete. (Herant Katchadourian, *Midlife in Perspective*)

The thing is, I don't *feel* like the middle-aged woman I am supposed to be. I feel as vital, as sexual, as I ever have. Perhaps more so, now that I am freed from the insecurities of my twenties and thirties, the need to be right, the need to please, to be approved of. The thing is, I'm finally old enough to have great fun flirting and fantasizing about playing around. It's not fair. Why should men have access to a pool of women that gets larger as they get older, while our pool shrinks with every passing day?

I'm recently separated. I want romance in my life. And romance for a woman in her fifties has a whole different meaning for me. You look in the mirror, and you see that you can't hold a candle to a woman who's thirty-six, in terms of a man's choices.

—Melva

It's funny for me to think that a thirty-year-old man would think of me as a fifty-year-old woman.

—Vivian

Of course, I know that not every middle-aged woman experiences this dissonance between how she feels on the inside and the way others perceive her. For some women, middle age brings relief from the need constantly to parry the male attention that comes from being sexually attractive. I have one friend, a young baby boomer, who is likely to be among that group. Extremely beautiful when she was young, she gained at least a hundred pounds after her divorce, when she was still in her early thirties. She once told me that she enjoyed the anonymity of being fat, because she no longer had constantly to fend off men. This friend is now in her forties. Maybe when she reaches fifty, she will allow herself to lose weight, protected by age from unwanted attention.

I understand my friend's point of view. But I'm not extraordinarily beautiful. I'm an ordinary woman and have had only my fair share of attention from the opposite sex. The loss of that attention is not a relief for me. It's a bitter pill. I've always enjoyed my sexuality and I am not ready to give it up.

Unfortunately, it doesn't seem to be my decision.

How many guys are sexually attracted to someone who is fifty years old ... somebody with their arms flapping and double chins and crepey neck and stuff ... (Grace Slick, *San Francisco Examiner,* August 17, 1989)

So much has changed for women over the years. I keep expecting the issue of sexual image to change as well. But it hasn't, and it probably won't. Warren Beatty, in his late fifties, marries thirty-something Annette Benning and no one blinks an eye. Elizabeth Taylor marries a younger man and the guffaws can be heard from coast to coast. We assume he's after her money; if not, he must be a pervert: "What's the matter, does he want to sleep with his *mother?*" One morning my eye was caught by a newspaper article that seemed to be about women who were married to younger men. Aha, I thought, a breakthrough, a new perspective on this subject that is becoming increasingly important to me. But to my disappointment, it was the same old thing, a list of men in their fifties, sixties, and seventies married to women in their twenties and thirties. I felt angry and betrayed.

Now we are told that even those in advanced old age are sexually far more active than we imagined them to be ... The image of an elderly couple dozing serenely side by side has been rehabilitated into one of tireless lovers copu-

lating the night away. (Herant Katchadourian, *Midlife in Perspective*)

It's a nice thought, but I don't think so, Dr. Katchadourian. Where are those rehabilitated images? As the baby boomers move into middle age, the question of sex after youth is much discussed, and experts seem to agree couples can and should happily continue sexual relations well into their golden years. But that doesn't mean people are comfortable with images of sex among the elderly, or that old women are in any way considered sexy. "Older" women may be elegant, beautiful, wise, witty, great fun, good friends—but they are certainly *not* sexy.

> *As I graduated into character parts in the eighties … one thing bothered me. There was never a love interest or sensual sensitivity in the roles I was playing … Did that mean that women in their fifties no longer were perceived as sexual beings?* (Shirley Maclaine, "Why I Don't Need a Man," excerpt from *Dance While You Can* in *McCall's*, November 1991)

> *They loved hearing about my sex life when I was married. But they didn't like hearing a fifty-two-year-old unmarried woman talking about dating and so forth. … They didn't want any innuendoes about sex from me.* (Joan Rivers on "Fresh Air," November 11, 1991)

In her book, *The Change*, Germaine Greer promotes the idea that women are better off once they have been "set free" from the need to make themselves sexually attractive. I don't disagree. I'm just not ready. I'm not looking for that level of freedom. But I know I must learn to live with it, just as I am learning to live with a body that doesn't like to stay awake too late or play tennis too long, hair that doesn't want to stay brown, skin that doesn't want to stay smooth and clear. I will learn to hide my feelings. I will learn to watch the movement of my eyes in the company of attractive men, especially if they're younger. I suppose I will learn, as the years go by, to accept the fact that I am becoming, in the eyes of the world, a sexless person.

But maybe I'm too pessimistic. Perhaps as large numbers of healthy, active women reach their fifties and sixties and seventies, ideas about sexual attractiveness will change. Older women are beginning to appear in the media, in commercials and ads, in films, as TV news anchors. We have re-invented ourselves in so many ways in terms of lifestyles and roles and careers and independence. Surely we can also re-invent ourselves in terms of our sexual image.

"GRANDMA?" WHO, ME?

My mother's death has left to me the grandmother's role for my family. Now I am the bearer of the family traditions. I will tell those important tales that link the old and the new. On long rainy nights I will tuck my grandsons in and tell them about growing up in the Bronx, or about how their grandma and grandpa met at college, or how we came west to San Anselmo. (Ethel Seiderman, *Fairfax/ San Anselmo Children's Center Newsletter,* Spring 1991)

The decrepit playground at the bottom of my hill, constructed when my children were toddlers and taken over in the Eighties by high school kids and drug dealers, has been transformed into a bright and shiny place for the neighborhood's newest generation. The children for whom the original playground was built are now having children of their own; last summer a group of young parents replaced the rotting redwood jungle gym with a blue and orange steel and plastic play structure, put down clean sand, and erected a nice green mesh fence to keep the dogs away. I watched them work as I drove up and down the hill. They all looked like kids to me.

My image of a fifty-year-old woman when I was growing up: an old dumpy schlepper ... a fat lady in a housedress with no makeup, no pride in herself, an apron, and grandchildren.

—Judy

My cousin, one year my junior, has a grandchild in elementary school. My friend Nancy, who straddles the line between my generation and the baby boomers, grins when she speaks of her four "grandbabies" and another on the way. Vivian is enthralled by her two grandchildren. I coo at babies in the supermarket, startled by the nostalgia that rises to the surface, and I have to admit that I wouldn't mind a part-time baby of my own. "Grandmother" has changed from something that I have, or had, to something I am in danger of becoming. Even though I cannot yet picture my children as parents, I assume that sooner or later I will hear myself addressed as "Grandma." Grandma? Who, me? Grandma is not me. Grandma was and will always be the thin wrinkled slow-moving warm loving funny woman who was my father's mother.

> *My grandson calls me Judy. I don't want him to call me Grandma. "I will be your grandmother," I say, "but you will call me 'Judy.'"*
>
> *—Judy*
>
> *Today's grandmothers don't look like grandmothers. They look like women.* (Lois Wyse, *Funny, You Don't Look Like a Grandmother*)

I had dinner recently with a grandmother who wore patterned leggings and an oversized sweater and huge flashy earrings. She looked fabulous. Most of the grandmothers I know divide their wardrobes between business suits, blue jeans, sweatpants and jogging shorts. They're slim, with stylish fifty-dollar haircuts, and they've traded in the family station wagon for a two-door sports car or a van in which they can haul skis and bicycles. As is our style, we are inventing our own grandma selves. It goes without saying that they hardly resemble the grandmas of our childhoods.

But the stereotypes persist. In his newspaper column, "Coming of Age," which ran for a few years in the *San Francisco Chronicle* Sunday magazine, historian Page Smith described grandmothers as having "soft and commodious laps ... who smell of lavender, bake cookies, and ... put things up." One reader's response echoed my own:

> Look around you, Page Smith: There are no rocking chairs
> ... these days ... See the grannies ... see the grannies at
> work. See the store-bought cookies in the cookie jar. Smell
> the smell of the new grandmother—it is sweat, not laven-
> der. (Betty McAfee, *San Francisco Chronicle*, December 1990)

I understand that you become the people who have been the touchstones in your life: "Mommy." "Grandma." That doesn't have to mean you are transformed into those people. Just because my grandmother wore little print dresses and hardly ever left the kitchen doesn't mean that's the way *I* have to be.

> I think society has changed, given us a whole new image
> of what women can be, that you don't have to be those
> stereotypes any more.
>
> —Judy

The information packet for my twenty-fifth high school reunion asked for the names and ages of *grandchildren*. But the grandmothers at that reunion, all closing in on fifty, didn't look as if they stayed home and baked cookies, and they smelled more of Chanel No. 5 than of lavender. The grandmothers in my parents' retirement community have traded in cookie baking for swimming and tennis and golf and amateur theatricals and cruises. Our children's storybooks might have led them to visualize Grandma in the kitchen baking cookies, but she was more likely to be waving goodbye from the driver's seat of a travel trailer or going off in her tailored suit to sell real estate.

So, just as the word "middle-aged" conjures up images that have little to do with the real thing, "grandma" is only a word. Judy doesn't have to worry about her grandchildren calling her "Grandma." Sticks and stones will break your bones but words will never hurt you. Anyway, *we're* the ones who decide what the word "grandma" means.

BUILDING

NEW MUSCLES

SEARCHING FOR HERO(INE)S

hero(ine): a woman admired and emulated for her achievements and qualities
role: a socially expected behavior pattern usually determined by an individual's status in a particular society
model: an example for imitation or emulation
                    (Webster's New World Dictionary, 1984)

I think what I really want ... I want to be my own hero. I think that's what I've been creating. Because there are no heroes out there. So I view the women I know as part of a huge supermarket, maybe a literary supermarket from which I can plagiarize, take a bit here and a bit there. I'll take a half a can of peas from her and a loaf of bread from her, and I'll incorporate it and change it and make it my own.
                                        —Susan

All the boys I grew up with were surrounded by heroes. Living heroes like General MacArthur and President Eisenhower. Historical heroes like Napoleon and Daniel Boone and George Washington and Christopher Columbus. Movie-star heroes like John Wayne. Fictional heroes like Prince Valiant and Tarzan and Superman and Sky King and Batman and the Lone Ranger. But who were we girls supposed to emulate? The blonde bimbos the boys' heroes saved? The boys' heroes' adoring wives and girlfriends? I never wanted to be Mamie Eisenhower, or Jane of the Jungle, or Lois Lane, or Bat*girl*, or Super*girl*. Except maybe for Wonder Woman, who acted alone and was pretty terrific, I can't remember one single woman I wanted to be when I grew up.

I liked Doris Day a lot. Nancy Drew. I really liked Cherry Ames. That's terrible, isn't it? Not to have any role models, any heroes? I liked Captain Video. I used to pretend we were married. He was Captain Video, and I was Margo, Queen of the World. But I was definitely his wife and he ruled the roost.
                                                    —Margo

I'm sure I had heroes. But I can't think of any. There are people I admire now, in my profession. There weren't any women role models when we were younger. I liked Tarzan.
                                                    —Anita

During the Fifties and Sixties, Doctor, Lawyer, and Indian Chief were always male. Women didn't run things. Women didn't publish newspapers or direct movies or fly airplanes or head up corporations or lead scientific research projects. Men ran the world, men made the big decisions, men did the important thinking. Women did the detail work, the nurturing, the caretaking. Cleaned up after the men. Wrote down their important thoughts. Reminded them about their important meetings. Protected them from interruptions while they did their important and mysterious business. My brother's role models were decision-makers and adventurers and leaders; mine were nurses and teachers, librarians and secretaries, waitresses and beauticians. And, of course, Wives and Mothers.

When I was in my twenties, I knew my friends' mothers, mostly immigrant mothers, Chinese or Japanese. Their interest in life was pretty much family. Ironing and getting the right kind of starch.
                                                    —Sachiko

My parents had very clear parameters. They knew what their roles were, and conflict that may have come around those roles was never really examined. Even my mother, who stepped outside those roles, always did it within the confines of wife, mother, a pillar of society. So whatever else she did, she did sort of on the Q.T., would race out, do it, and race back in again and cover herself up with the camouflage of being acceptable, with propriety.

—Susan

Even if you had a mother who worked outside the home, even though you saw many women who worked, some of whom were professionals or in positions of authority, the Primary Message rang loud and clear from every television show, movie, magazine, and book, from parents and teachers and school counselors and family friends: Boys should aspire to the Presidency; girls should aspire to marry the man who would become President, have two-point-five well-behaved children, maintain a beautiful home, and greet poor tired hubby at the door each evening with a smile, a freshly bathed and powdered body, and a very dry martini. If you felt, deep down, that something was wrong with that picture, everything and everyone conspired to tell you that there was something wrong with *you.*

We were always feeling off balance, slightly out of place, like you didn't get it. Whatever the convention was, you didn't get it. Or couldn't do it.

—Susan

My way of behaving, of *being*, constantly evoked disapproval. I was too loud. I always tried to be first. I had no interest in learning to cook. I hated to shop. I loved being in charge. I loved to compete. I loved to win. I wanted everyone to know how smart I was. I was certainly not ladylike. I was certainly not content to sit back and wait to be called on in class. Not willing to give in when I thought I was right. I was definitely out of step. Troublesome. By the age of eight or nine I knew that I wanted something else out of life than what I was supposed to have. I wanted to be someone other than who I was supposed to be. I couldn't have said who that was, but I did know that she was certainly not my mother.

When Ken and I moved to Ann Arbor, I joined a women's group. I had a lot of women role models in this group, women who were very articulate, very bright, also from Asian Women's organizations. I began to see that a lot of my ideas of what I could be or couldn't be came from the fact that I didn't have role models as a child.

—Sachiko

I have several role models now: Katharine Hepburn and Lauren Bacall. Katharine Hepburn—her tenacity—she didn't care what the world thought, and she carried it off with grace and charm. She was way ahead of her time. Independent. She didn't need to make herself a whole person by marrying somebody. Lauren Bacall, because she's a brassy, classy dame. Again, strong, independent. The image she portrays is one of "Knock me down and I'll get right back up again, and don't try to knock me down again because you won't succeed." And I admire that. When I was a kid and would go to my friends' houses and meet their families, there was usually a dynamic, eccentric woman somewhere. Not a mother. A grandmother or an aunt. And I loved her.

—Judy

When towards the end of the Sixties and in the early Seventies the women I knew began talking to one another about subjects other than boys and clothes and children and wallpaper, it turned out that many of us had always felt out of step. The women we had admired most during our formative years were not our mothers but the women people laughed at or talked about in whispers. The women everyone considered "strange." We may not have known why we admired them, but we sensed they knew something we hadn't figured out yet. Now I see that what we must have admired was the way they knew very well how they were supposed to behave—they just didn't give a damn.

> *There was one gray-haired lady in my community, a widow. She lived by herself. Worked as a communicator for the Federal Aviation Agency. And when she had her days off, she really got off on us kids. She would take us blueberry picking. I used to love to talk to her. She had this extensive garden, and she had these poppies. She said, "See those poppies?" I said, "Yeah." And she said, "Opium poppies." I said, "Really? Isn't that against the law?" And she said, "Oh, I'm not supposed to have them. But if the agricultural agent comes by, I'll just do the little gray-haired old lady routine."*
>
> *—Betty*

Just as we had jettisoned our bras and stopped trying to iron the curls out of our hair, we were more than ready to toss out the traditional models of the way we were supposed to be. But we were working with a negative: We knew who we *didn't* want to emulate, but we had little to choose from when seeking replacements. "Hero" still meant "man."

There are very few older women who are seen as com-
pelling role-models for young women. We have a few hero-
ines, but not enough yet. I was talking to two friends ...
and we all had to say ... that most of the figures we
wove our ambitions around were men. (Elizabeth Janeway,
Between Myth and Morning: Women Awakening)

My heroes and role models are male. There are many
women I admire. My mentors have all been women. But
my heroes and role models are male.

—*Anita*

I've been inspired by men, in terms of "That's the way I
want to be, that's a possibility." But I can't think of any
women when I was growing up who played that role.

—*Vivian*

We didn't want to be men. We just didn't want to be like
most of the women we had known. We searched for role models,
women who did and said surprising things, who did the unexpected, who made "difficult" choices and made them work. We
found them in our families, in our schools, in our communities.

I met a woman named Emma Stern who must have been
in her late sixties or early seventies. She was very bright,
and she was very much involved with civil rights. She'd
been born in the South, and at Smith College she met
W.E.B. Du Bois at a luncheon, and she had a very heated
debate about slavery and blacks. And from that time on,
she began to think about it. She married a conventional
southern gentleman and moved to New York. While he
went off to work, she'd have civil rights meetings at her
house. Later they moved to California and she continued

doing a lot of political work. She was involved with the Jackson Five and died just about that time. I admired her a lot. I thought, "Here she is all wrinkled, she has five or six jowls, and yet there's this wonderful life coming out of her."

—*Sachiko*

My first minority teacher in my life was Sarah Lawrence Lightfoot. She was a little younger than me. She transformed my life. At one point she told me I had an easily colonized mind. My whole reality expanded.

—*Betty*

I found my first real female role model at college, a professor my mother's age who was everything my mother seemed not to be. In her early forties when her marriage ended in divorce, she returned to school and earned a Ph.D. Then she moved from the Midwest to San Francisco—almost a foreign country—and took a teaching position at San Francisco State. This was in the early Sixties, when divorce was rare and divorced women were expected to live quietly on alimony or take a respectable job, not draw attention to themselves, and pray they could attract a nice widower. But Arlen wasn't interested. She was loud and sure of herself and brilliant. She took stage, as they say, all the time. She made her share of enemies, partly because she would not tolerate dullness or stupidity and didn't much care whether people liked her. It was respect she wanted, and it was respect she got. She was the first grownup woman I had ever known who said, "This is what I'm going to do," and did it, without seeming to care "what people would think." I didn't know you could do that and get away with it. In the years that followed, I carried her image with me for strength, and I told her story again and again. She opened doors for me, doors I hadn't even seen, and helped me see the possibilities.

> We are without role models, cutting a new path yet one more time in our lives. I thought it was one thing to come out to San Francisco and be a single parent, and then to be a single working parent, and then to be a single working parent who was going to school, and then to be a single working parent going to school who might be having an affair, and so each time I was attempting something new. It felt like, maybe, Charles Atlas building new muscles.
>
> —Susan

> Emma was my first friend who was old, and she was a good role model for me, someone who was still active. Meeting her gave me an idea that life didn't end at thirty or forty. And I thought about what it would be like to be Emma's age. I would have wanted to say that I did what I wanted to do, that I tried, instead of saying, "I could have been ... "
>
> —Sachiko

As I enter my own middle age I begin again to seek role models, heroes who can show me what is possible, and I think again of Arlen. I feel comforted when I recall that at the age of sixty, when most people are planning their retirement, she recreated herself again by going back to school for a law degree and building a new career in immigration law. Today, in her eighties and widowed from her second (younger) husband, she teaches at a San Francisco law school—and is madly in love again. Her life is still unfolding.

If it is suggested to the older woman that she should start out toward a new future, she will sadly reply that it is too late. Not that henceforth her time is limited, for a woman goes into retirement very early; but she lacks the spirit, the confidence, the hope, the anger, that would enable her to look around and find new goals. (Simone de Beauvoir, *The Second Sex*)

I think we're lucky. We have a lot of women right now who are in their fifties and sixties who are well respected, who look great, who are full of energy.

—Marlene

Arlen and women like her are heroes to my generation because they were willing to risk being themselves, willing to go against the norm, to do what they wanted and needed to do within a society that pursed its collective lips in disapproval. They helped change the perception that a women's role *must* be limited, that women *must* behave in a certain way. They also gave lie to the almost universally held belief that a woman "of a certain age" has reached the end of her useful life. They proved, instead, that middle age can be a time of exciting new beginnings, that we can create ourselves, and recreate ourselves, as often as we want. We don't need anyone's permission.

WOMAN'S WORK

It is through gainful employment that woman has traversed most of the distance that separated her from the male, and nothing else can guarantee her liberty in practice. (Simone de Beauvoir, *The Second Sex*)

My father was theoretically a feminist, but when it came to the nitty gritty ... he expected everything to be done for him by ... his wife. It was taken for granted that "his work" must come before everything else. (May Sarton, *Journal of a Solitude*)

May Sarton was writing of her family in the early part of this century. She might as well have been writing of 1956, or 1964. Here is a 1964 photograph of the nine University of California chancellors: nine white men in identical dark suits, white shirts, and narrow dark ties. Here are photographs of the leading radicals of the Free Speech movement. Yes, they are long-haired and shaggy. Yes, they've replaced their suits and ties with jeans or chinos, workshirts, and beads. But they are all white men. The women of the Movement cluster around them. The women cook the food, take notes, gaze with adoration at their men while they speak, stay slightly behind, slightly lower.

As I think back over the span of my life (and shake my head in wonder as I realize I am reviewing more than half a century), what comes to mind is the enormous change in what is perceived to be "women's work." When I graduated from college in 1964, I could be (and was) a secretary. I could be (and was) a proofreader and copy editor. I could be (and was) a teacher. I could be (and was) a sales clerk. I could have opened a shop (I did). I could have become a real estate agent (which I considered), an administrative assistant, a social worker, a librarian, a nurse, an office manager, a housekeeper, a travel agent, a bookkeeper, a bank teller, a waitress, a dental hygienist, or a court reporter. But I would have been strongly discouraged—or even barred—from becoming a(n):

airline pilot	fireman
symphony conductor	sports reporter
CEO of a corporation	state governor
bank manager	auto mechanic
surgeon	managing editor of a major
engineer	newspaper
architect	big city mayor
member of the Cabinet	judge
pharmacist	police detective
carpenter	president of a major
construction worker	university
chemist	rabbi
attorney	minister
dentist	film director
TV anchor	senator

and ... and ... and ...

I recently spent some time in the corridors of the University of California medical school. My age shows when I say that I was surprised that many of the women I met there were medical students. Not technicians or nurses in training, but women who were studying to be doctors. Women did not study medicine when I was young; I didn't have a woman doctor until I was in my twenties, and even then it was rare. The only woman my age I knew who became a doctor had two small children when she made up her mind to go to medical school: "It's something I've always wanted," she told me, "and I finally realized that it was something I could do." I think my parents hoped that my brother might become a doctor, or a lawyer, but I never recall them voicing such aspirations for me. I would have liked to be a lawyer, and I would probably have been a good one. But no one, parent, aunt or uncle, teacher or high school counselor, ever suggested law as an avenue for me, except to impress on me that legal secretaries made good money. Today, close to half the members of a typical law school class are women.

> *I think what's most important is the changing status of women. I remember how woodshop was for boys and clothing was for girls, and not seeing anything wrong with that. As a result I never went on in math, which I enjoyed. It's an incredible difference between then and now, when women are encouraged to go into everything, and supported.*
>
> *—Anita*

Math, science, business, the professions—all men. Government. All men. When I was growing up, the only women I saw in government were the ones who wrote down the men's words or stood next to (and a little behind) them to demonstrate spousal support as they made campaign speeches. Today, both California senators are women. Two women sit on the Supreme Court. A woman is attorney general. Great Britain and India and Bangladesh have or have had female prime ministers. Women are judges, mayors, governors, cabinet members. Who would have thought it possible?

In the Fifties, mommies had to come home from the factories and pamper people and cook soup and vacuum in high heels (just in case a Better Homes and Gardens photographer should stop by). There was no recognition of women as equal partners.
—Marlene

What everyone seems to forget is that women have *always* worked. Single women and poor married women have always had to hold down jobs in addition to housekeeping and caretaking. Not having to work, "to be taken care of," was a mark of success. And even though we daughters of affluent middle-class families were never expected to have to support ourselves in the larger sense, we were still subject to the work ethic. We were expected to earn our own spending money and support ourselves until we made a "good" marriage. But you never know, and you should always be prepared. So at my parents' urging, I took typing and shorthand in summer school. Those "women's" skills did come in useful for landing temporary and part-time jobs while I was in college. But once I'd graduated, I quickly learned that when I applied for a job, *any* job, the first question would be, "How fast can you type?" and my answer had to be, "Sorry. No can do." Because if people knew I could type or take shorthand or use the Xerox machine or make coffee, that's what I'd end up doing.

When I became a lawyer in 1965 and started looking for a job, it was hopeless. People would say, "We called you in because we wanted to see what a lady lawyer looked like." When I finally got a job, I concealed my second pregnancy. I wore a girdle, and I wasn't pregnant until I was seven months along, and I took my girdle off and said, "Guess what!" Afterwards, I went back to work immediately.
—Anita

When Anita and I entered the job market, it was taken for granted that (1) women should not take jobs away from men who needed them to feed their families, (2) certain jobs were inappropriate for women, (3) women were not intellectually or emotionally or physically suited for certain jobs, (4) men should be in charge, and (5) women would quit work when they married, or at least when they got pregnant. Despite the interlude of World War II, when women "bravely" stepped in to keep the country moving while men went off to the front (and were quickly pushed out when the men returned), nothing had changed since Margo's mother began working in the late Thirties.

> *My mother went NYU in science, pre-med. I think her field was medical research, or biology. But she ended up at Macy's. You weren't allowed to be married. ... you couldn't take a job away from a man who had to support a family, so she never told them she was married. She worked in the coat department, and she was pregnant with Richard, and one day her supervisor said, "Miss Jacobson, are you pregnant?" And she was so humiliated she ran out and never cashed her last paycheck.*
>
> —Margo

> *All my parents wanted me to do was get through high school. If I wanted to go to college, there had to be some practical reason. So I told them I was going to teach. They figured I should marry a professional, a doctor or lawyer. My mother thought the best thing would be for me to go to secretarial school so I could learn some skills, make a living if I had to. My mother didn't go beyond eighth grade, so she thought just graduating from high school was wonderful.*
>
> —Sachiko

Education changed things. The generation of women who came of age in the Fifties and early Sixties was raised with the idea that "a good education" was the ticket to a good life, although how a good education was defined differed widely. I'd known since the age of four that my parents expected me to go to college. For the children of immigrants, their families didn't have much money and college was a luxury, especially for girls. So they believed that a college education was the ticket for their own children. A college education meant you'd arrived, although the destination remained vague. My parents weren't alone. All the bright middle-class women I knew were expected to go to college. After all, where else were we to find suitable husbands? Well, it sure was a mistake to send so many women to college—it made us uppity in numbers that had never been seen before.

> *I think the interesting thing for us is that in almost every year of our lives we were striking new molds, breaking new ground. We've figured out that it's going to be different. I don't think we decided. I think there were a lot of social and economic forces as a result of the Second World War. It takes a long time. You throw the rock in the pool, and there's a ripple, and it goes on and on.*
>
> —Marlene

> *I guess in a way, to be a thinking intellectual honest-to-God Indian egghead, to be able to think grownup thoughts, to be able to have that latitude, to be working in a supportive environment, that has transformed my life. [Without Women's Lib and the Civil Rights Movement] I think my life would have been one of extreme frustration. I don't think I would have lived very long. Being able to do my scholarly work … I never dreamed that I could do*

this. It's really neat. I can't imagine being able to cope
without it. In a sense, going to Harvard, I had to do it.

—Betty

It seems simple, looking back (everything seems simple, looking back). We had been raised to be independent and confident.
We knew we could earn enough money to get by on our own, so
we didn't have to marry the first man who came along or stay in
an intolerable marriage. For whatever reasons, we didn't want or
weren't good at living the lives our mothers had lived. For whatever reasons, we wanted something more. Something different.
So we applied for jobs we weren't supposed to have. We went to
law school and medical school. We got MBAs. We borrowed language and ideas and strategies from the Civil Rights Movement
and demanded to be treated equally in the work force. When we
got pregnant, we refused to quit our jobs; we took off a couple of
weeks, put our kids in day care, and went right back to work—
with or without our husbands' "permission." In less than twenty-
five years, we've changed the character of "women's work" and
the nature of the American work force. It hasn't been easy. But
we had no choice.

The women who are getting more into mid-management
have pretty diminished social lives, and the few that have
children, their children are entirely cared for by other people.
What's quality time at seven at night after a day in day
care? It's true, the options for women in the business world
have expanded somewhat, but they're still not real well
paid, and it's pretty difficult if they want a husband and
children. It's a pretty frantic, nervous life, and one thing or
the other is going to suffer.

—Lynn

It's hard enough physically for a woman to continue being a teacher or physicist after she's had a child, but emotionally it's hardest of all: She runs the intolerable risk of being called not independent but selfish, or, most biting of all, masculine. Women who do creative work at home have equal problems because there's no uninterruptible time and they're socialized to respond to every household crisis, no matter how trivial. We move from guilt to guilt, damned if we do, and damned if we don't. (Dorothy Gilman, A New Kind of Country)

Now that women are in the work force in large numbers, and in positions that matter, our attempts to balance the demands of our personal lives with the demands of our careers have opened a new dialogue about the nature of work, a dialogue that has implications not only for women but for men. I run training programs for corporations, and I often kick off the first session with the question, "What would you do with the time if you were given a six-month leave with full pay?" When I started asking that question ten years ago, men would usually say, "Travel," or "Go fishing," while women would be likely to respond, "Spend more time with my kids." Over the past three or four years, men have also started to say that they would like to spend more time with their kids. I know both women and men who have turned down promotions or promising jobs that meant increased traveling or longer hours, others who have taken unpaid leaves to devote time to their families or their personal growth, and many who have negotiated full- or part-time work-at-home arrangements with employers—more flexible work styles that acknowledge personal and family needs.

The past decade has seen a powerful counterassault on women's rights, a backlash, an attempt to retract the handful of small and hard-won victories that the feminist movement did manage to win for women. (Susan Faludi, *Backlash: The Undeclared War Against American Women*)

Women are still far from equal in the workplace. Women must still engage in the great American juggling act just to get through the day. Tough economic times and uncertain family structures force today's young women to juggle even harder than we did. The "glass ceiling" is still a brick wall for many women in business and the professions; women architects must team up with men to get commissions; women attorneys still have to fight for partnerships in law firms. Only a handful of women head large corporations, and most of the faces on corporate boards are still those of wealthy white men. Women surgeons are still harassed in medical schools. Women who are bright enough and assertive enough to make their way to the top are still accused of being controlling and domineering and bitchy. And traditional "women's work," nursing, teaching, administering, caretaking, is still underpaid and undervalued. Nevertheless, we have seen real, sweeping, lasting changes for American women, changes in the fabric of our society, changes that are starting to ripple through other cultures. It's exciting to think that we have raised daughters who assume they will participate in the world on an equal footing with men. Daughters who expect to be taken seriously. Daughters who see possibilities for themselves that women of our generation could only dimly imagine.

Now I see this ... great life-enhancing revolution, still not finished, but having enormously changed the possibilities for all women ... slowed to a halt by the general reversal of social progress in America in the dozen years of the Reagan and Bush administrations. (Betty Freidan, "The Dangers of the New Feminine Mystique," *McCall's*, November 1991)

My generation, the women who married in the early or middle Sixties, may be the last to have a choice between career and family, the last with the possibility of saying, "Then I stopped what I was doing and raised my kids." We may also be the last generation of women who were able to reach for the stars without worrying overmuch about whether we got there. When we took ourselves out of the house into the world of work, *anything* we did was an accomplishment. We knew the obstacles were there; we expected them, and we found solidarity in our struggle against them. Today, young women expect—and are expected—to have a career; they must deal with the same pressures to succeed as men while confronting the subtle and not so subtle obstacles continually placed in their path. As Betty Freidan says, these young women do not consider themselves feminists. They thought the revolution was over. They thought feminism was history and they are surprised to find that the barriers are still up.

As the Republican majority in Congress gleefully slashes away at the rights of everyone who is not rich, white, male and powerful, the "revolution" is bound to slow even further, and some hardwon ground might well be lost. Maybe I'm a starry-eyed optimist, but I think it's important to recognize the real gains. My daughter considers herself a *person* first and a woman second. She will never define herself primarily as someone's wife and someone's mother. She will be less likely to eliminate possibilities for herself based on whether they constitute "women's work." She will have to make choices to balance work and family, and she may decide at some point to defer her career while she raises children—but it will be *her* decision. That is our real achievement, opening up the world for our daughters. And we have an additional responsibility: We need to keep telling the story of what it was like *before*, so our daughters understand how their lives are different because of what we have done and how they, too, have the power and responsibility to change what needs to be changed, to make things different, for their own children and the generations to come.

WE CAN TAKE CARE OF OURSELVES!

I remember when I got married, and we were in a motel room in Elko, Nevada. I was washing out Tom's socks, and I remember thinking, "This is it. I'm married and taking care of my husband." And I felt depressed. It was as if any desires I had from that time on were secondary. I think that's the way we thought it was supposed to be. I remember when I got back from Bolivia, about four years later. And Tom said, "There are two things I'll never understand: the Women's Movement and astrology." This was 1969. December of 1969.

—Margo

I cannot understand women who look with distaste at the women's movement; my God, I think, where have they been? (Dorothy Gilman, *A New Kind of Country*)

In my more lucid moments, I wonder what would have become of me if someone hadn't invented Women's Lib, if women like Betty Freidan and Simone de Beauvoir and Liv Ullman and Gloria Steinem, and even Jane Fonda, had not articulated my frustrations, had not made it possible to say, "Wait a minute. This isn't the way I have to be."

I was married to a man who was very controlling. Even when I was married to him, I said, "I'd like to go to school," but he didn't want me to. He gave me one check at a time for the groceries. He was so controlling that I lost all my self-esteem. I couldn't even think for myself. He'd make all the decisions. Even when the children would ask if they could stay overnight at somebody's house, I'd have to ask him. I married him because I wanted to be taken care of.

—*Maureen*

I just thought that was what I was supposed to do. Marriage was expected, and it was final and forever.

—*Margo*

One of the so-called "revolutionary" acts of the Sixties and early Seventies was to jettison the traditional words of the marriage ceremony: "Who *gives* this woman ... " "Love, honor, and *obey* ... " Those words appeared to validate the concept of woman as possession, woman as an immature, inferior being incapable of making decisions or taking responsibility for herself, incapable of growing up. Destined to remain innocent and dependent, to pass from the care of father to the care of husband, to remain "barefoot and pregnant in the kitchen" while the man took care of worldly matters, handled the money, did the thinking and the planning. And not only is that what society expected of us, it was *we* expected for ourselves. What we *wanted*. Anything less was failure.

Although nothing was ever said of marriage being the best and only route for women, my mother's voice would change when she spoke of unmarried women. "X is so very nice ... and really so attractive that I wonder why she's never married." Presumably there had to be something deficient, something flawed there ... like a fruit that looks luscious on the outside but has rot inside. The antenna picks up these signals early. (Dorothy Gilman, *A New Kind of Country*)

My mother was crazed. My mother had two of us who weren't "moving." (Joan Rivers on "Fresh Air," November 8, 1991)

Of course, the desire to set up housekeeping with a mate and share the experience of raising a family spans the generations. Now in their mid-twenties, my daughter and her friends are glancing anxiously at the biological clock, and one by one they are forming serious relationships. But it was different for us. We didn't just *want* to marry, we *had* to marry. If you weren't married by twenty-two or twenty-three, people (read "mothers") began to worry. If you were still single at twenty-five or twenty-six, they talked about you in lowered voices. God forbid you should still be a spinster at thirty. So what that your family was progressive, that you wore pants, that you smoked and drank in bars. So what that you graduated from college, had a good job and supported yourself (in an apartment shared with girlfriends). All that was superficial. Temporary. Only marriage would validate you in the eyes of society—and in the eyes of your mother. Almost every woman I knew honestly believed that her destiny was to get married to Mr. Right and make the marriage work. The worst thing you could do was fail to find someone to marry; a close second was to fail at *being* married. Marriage was the way you defined yourself as a woman and as a person. And marriage was your security. Without it, you had nothing.

This is the first time I've lived alone. The first night I woke up in the middle of the night, thought I was choking to death. I got in my car, went to the emergency room, and I said, I'm afraid I'm going to suffocate in my sleep because I can't breathe. The doctor checked my lungs, my heart, and he said, I think you're having an anxiety attack. I said, you mean I'm not going to die? He said, well, not from this. I got back in my car and went home. It was the

*strangest, strangest feeling. I never knew I would feel that
way, because I've always been so independent.*

—*Melva*

*What frightens me most—and this goes back to the con-
vention of the 1950s—is that I was supposed to be taken
care of. And that meant forever. And that meant medical
bills, and insurance, and taken care of. And that's not
present.*

—*Susan*

But women have *always* managed on their own! My great-
grandmother, a widow, ran a boarding house to support herself
and her children. Widows, abandoned wives, wives with husbands
who were sick or lazy or too unskilled to find work, spinsters—
they've always found ways to take care of themselves and their
children. So where did this fantasy come from, this image of women
as helpless, immature creatures who need to be take care of? And
why did we buy into it?

*Girls were supposed to be helpmates and good mothers,
and somehow that didn't appeal to me. My mother was
always complaining about being stuck at home. I must
have taken that very seriously, because I thought, "I'm not
going to be stuck at home."*

—*Sachiko*

My mother exemplifies the "traditional" woman. She's never
lived alone. She hasn't worked outside the home since she got
married. She didn't go to college. She was in her mid-thirties when
she learned to drive, and I don't think she has ever driven on a
freeway. She knows a little bookkeeping, because she helped my
father run his musical contracting business. She can balance a
checkbook (which is more than Leslie could do when her first
husband separated). But my father has always paid the bills and

managed the money, and while he was hospitalized for six agonizing weeks during which we didn't know from day to day whether he would survive, I would find her at his desk late at night reading and re-reading invoices and bank statements and ledger sheets, trying to make sense of them. My mother has always been taken care of; that was what she expected and what she wanted. At eighty, it's the only way she knows how to live.

> When I started teaching in the mid-Seventies, I was still getting, "Oh, I'm just a housewife, all I've done is raise three kids and help my husband with his career, that's all I know." Women discount their reality from thirty to seventy percent. We have a lot of automatic "duck and cover" behaviors we use to put ourselves down. It's really hard to unlearn these behaviors.
> —Betty

When I was in my teens and early twenties, I used to watch my mother puttering around the house and wonder, "What in the world does she do with herself all day? Isn't she bored? Does she think a thought that my father hasn't already expressed?" But when I'd ask, "Gee, Mom, isn't there something else you wanted to do with your life?" she'd shrug. "Once I thought I'd like to be a hairdresser," she'd say, or "I would have liked to be a dancer, but your grandfather disapproved." More often, "Don't be ridiculous, Janis, I'm fine." She was probably telling the truth, but it was hard for me to believe that she didn't want *something* more. When my brother left and she clearly had little to do, I'd make suggestions. "Why don't you take some classes," I'd say. "Why in the world would I want to do that," she'd respond, adding, "I'm fine, Janis. Don't worry about me." I finally gave up and stopped pushing, but I renewed my contract with myself to have a different sort of life … somehow.

When I got married, I was a housewife trying very hard to be an artist. One year I made banana bread and wrapped it up in gift wrap and gave it to my friends. They would say, "Coming from you, this is very special." And I realized that I had this image of myself as a housewife, but it wasn't the image people had of me. I could hardly do the dishes. I remember hemming Ken's pants and taking an hour to do each leg. Ken expected me to be just like his mother, who was a perfect housewife. Mothers of that generation just did it, and were so good at it. Maybe they were just resigned to it. In Japanese culture, your roles are so clearly defined. That, superimposed on American culture, makes you crazy.

—Sachiko

It's tricky, trying to re-cast yourself. I like to consider myself a feminist. I like to think that I have freed myself from dependency. After all, I've always worked. I never felt I needed to ask my husband's permission when I wanted to do something. I've always managed the money in our family and made big decisions. I've lived on my own and know that I am perfectly capable of taking care of myself. And yet, when our first child was born, I automatically assumed the wife/mother/housekeeper role as my primary responsibility. It was not something my husband and I discussed; I simply assumed the role, as if I had been born to it. Before Jennifer was born, I'd told everyone at work I'd be back in a couple of weeks, but once she was part of my life, it seemed wrong to abandon her to the care of others, just like everyone around me said. So I stayed home, nursing the baby, washing diapers, cleaning house, and cooking dinner for my hubby. That was my happy homemaker stage, which lasted for all of six months. When the walls started closing in, I took a part-time job, forcing myself to ignore stabs of guilt when I left Jennifer at the babysitter's. Then one evening, she refused to leave the babysitter's arms. The next morning, I called my pediatrician in a panic: "I'm hurting my baby by leaving her with someone else, aren't I?" To my great good fortune, he laughed and told me to read Kate Millet and Germaine Greer. I kept the job and took on more, but as I juggled work and family over the next twenty years, I was careful to make sure that whatever job I had *never* got in the way of my real work: Raising my children and running my household.

> *When we first met, Bob was making tacos, and I said,*
> *"Oh, don't do that, I'll cook." And he said, "Fine," and he*
> *never cooked again. I realize now that that was because*
> *I wouldn't let him.*
>
> *—Margo*

You weren't only expected to see wife/mother/housekeeper as your primary role, you were expected to play that role perfectly. I have a vivid memory of my aunt and mother dissecting my cousin Judy's housekeeping. Judy married right out of high school and had two children by the time she was twenty. "Her place is filthy!" my aunt complained, adding quickly, "She certainly didn't learn that from me." "Kids," my mother said, shaking her head. Not many years later I tried not to notice as my father brushed dog hair off his trousers with barely disguised irritation and my mother worked to keep her face impassive as her eyes registered the layer of dust on our bookshelves. "So what?" I thought. So I wasn't much of a housekeeper. My kids were clean and well-fed, the beds got changed regularly, and the floor was kept clear of anything that might choke a toddler. So dog hair and dust weren't high on my list of priorities. Everything that was really important got done. That was my primary job, after all, no matter what else I might be doing. My husband, being liberated, "helped" with the shopping and the cleaning and the child care—as long as I told him what needed to be done. That was only fair. He was the provider; my various jobs and businesses brought in only an irregular supplementary income. We had tacitly agreed that his primary responsibility was income-provider, and mine was wife/mother/housekeeper. That's why I couldn't work full time. And anyway, wasn't I the one who was supposed to be taken care of?

It was interesting to see how the roles changed as the kids got older. By the time they left, my primary activities were outside the home, and my husband and I were sharing most of the household duties. Little by little I let go of my need to pretend I was keeping up with the household tasks. I all but stopped cooking and made only desultory stabs at keeping things in order. Again with no discussion, my husband stepped in to fill the void. Today, he's far more likely to plan meals and cook than I am, more likely to notice what needs to be cleaned and clean it. He does most of the shopping, because he cares the most about the food. He's so good at this new role that I can't help speculate how our lives might have been different if I'd had the career and he'd stayed home. But that option didn't exist for us. He grew up expecting to have a wife, and I grew up expecting to *be* a wife.

My daughter moved to Fairbanks for high school when I was forty. I bought the little condo in South City, and it was the first time in my life that I had lived alone. I went into shock. People kept saying, "Thank God you're liberated." I would go home after work, and by 7:00 I'd be climbing the walls. And then I realized, I don't have to go home. And I found myself doing things for other people that don't have to be done. If my children are there, I think I should cook. And my daughter said, "You know, I

*feed myself now, Mom." It puts me in a real crisis mode
to stop and think, "What do I want to do?"*

—Betty

The roles we are taught to play dictate so much about our behavior, what's okay and what's not okay, who gets to do what, who gets what. I heard recently that the word "chairman" comes from a time when a household might have only one real chair. The man got the chair, while the women and children crowded onto benches. "That was a long, long time ago, I thought." The next day I opened a magazine to a picture of a family with seven children, a family of the Nineties, with supposedly modern ideas about who is who. In the photograph, the father sits in a large comfortable armchair, surrounded by his wife and children—standing. I think about supposedly minor differences in behavior between the men and the women I know. My husband and my father and my brother can sit down in an armchair and fall asleep in ten seconds. Most women can't do that. It's hard enough for us to sit down without something in our hands; we feel guilty if we're not doing something productive. (My mother keeps a bag of knitting or crocheting or, most recently, needlepoint, next to her television chair.) Certainly when you have young children and a partner and a house to care for, you have little time to rest, and your work day certainly doesn't end at five o'clock. But I think the constant busyness reflects how we see ourselves: Who are we if not the tasks we do? I think of a neighbor who went a little crazy. She was the mother of five children born within six years. One afternoon she arrived at my house to pick up her seven-year-old son, carrying a loaf of French bread and a knife. We sat at my kitchen table chatting about this and that while the boys played in the yard. As we talked, she methodically cut the loaf of bread into neat, even slices and slipped them into a paper bag. When she was through she held the bag up, smiled brightly, and said, "For dinner." After she'd gone, I sat down and read a book.

My neighbor had stepped perilously close to the edge—who wouldn't, with five little kids? Yet even though her behavior seemed extreme, it wasn't (and still isn't) unusual. As women, we've been taught not to take time for ourselves, at least not until we've taken care of everyone else's real and perceived needs. Then maybe, just maybe, we can take a bubble bath. I think of the scene in the film "Peggy Sue Got Married" where Kathleen Turner's mother hovers around the table while the rest of the family eats. That was my mother, my grandmother, my aunts, my friends' mothers. Watching television is an opportunity to iron and fold laundry. Sitting down to rest or chat with a friend is a chance to knit, or mend, or polish the silver, or slice the French bread for supper.

> I came to believe that responsibility defines me as a person. If my house were clean and my refrigerator were full, and I tended to the needs of others, then I was an okay person. And I can't quite put that down yet. It bothers me a whole bunch.
>
> —Susan

Family legend has it that both of my grandmothers suffered "nervous breakdowns" when their children were in their teens. The reasons were unclear. My father's mother had always been anxious and nervous; she'd had a difficult life. My mother blamed her wayward older brother for her mother's "breakdown." "He made her sick, Janis. You don't know." Whatever the reasons, the fact that these women had "breakdowns" is hardly surprising. How else are you going to get any peace and quiet if you aren't allowed to take care of yourself, if you are overworked and have to be perfect all the time? How else are you going to get any rest? My friends and I run off to therapists when life becomes overwhelming; our grandmothers had no such options, so breakdowns were the obvious choice. If you lose control, someone else has to take over. Someone else has to step in and do the cooking and the laundry and care for the children and make the clothes and scrub the floors while you go away to rest or hide out in your bedroom with the shades drawn.

> *I was always brainwashed by my mother and aunts that anything you did to promote yourself, to improve yourself, was bad. I struggled with that for years. And I would always end up feeling guilty, and I was being selfish. And now ... I don't have to do that any more.*
>
> —*Melva*

Women no longer need breakdowns to justify a rest. The world doesn't fall apart if we say no, if we go for a bike ride or get a facial or take a nap or go to a movie instead of cleaning out the closets on our day off. Our grandmothers still live within us, it's true, and despite Kate Millet and Betty Freidan and Gloria Steinem, despite years of therapy, we haven't completely succeeded in dislodging the guilt, in quieting the little voice that mutters, "Selfish, selfish," when we do something for ourselves. But more of us are able to ignore that nagging voice more of the time. More of us are giving our daughters the message that it's okay to take care of yourself. It's okay to take time for what pleases and refreshes you and helps you grow, and to put your own needs first some of the time. It's okay to call attention to your achievements and value yourself. It's healthy and it's good.

SINGLE AT FIFTY

I think it's very different being single and being fifty than being married and being fifty. I never dreamed I wouldn't spend my life in a relationship with someone. We were raised to think that marriage was forever. And that's not the reality. Divorce became more common when women found out that they can take care of themselves.

—Judy

A mobilization usually begins in the late forties that registers with rising exhilaration as women move into their fifties. They drop happy face masks. They break the seal on their repressed anger. They overcome habits of trying to be perfect and make everyone love them. They often shed the terror of living without a man. (Gail Sheehy, *Pathfinders*)

When I was growing up, single woman were to be pitied. It didn't matter why they were single—never married, divorced, or widowed—and it didn't matter whether they were thirty or fifty or seventy. The assumption was that a woman needed a husband, and that was all there was to it. Today, although people still make that assumption more often than not, living as a single woman has become a viable option. Not the best option for every woman, even not the best option for most, but *possible* in a way that it wasn't for our mothers and grandmothers.

For one thing, we're far more independent financially. We can earn enough to support ourselves and our children, if we must, because we have access to more lucrative jobs. We can get credit cards in our own names (my husband had to co-sign for my first credit card, in 1976). We can take out loans to purchase property (my brother and sister-in-law were denied a loan in 1969 because she was the one with the well-paying job). We know how to balance our checking accounts and manage our expenses. We are more independent in other ways as well. We can negotiate with salespeople. We can deal with the plumber and the electrician and the auto mechanic. We know, as well as anyone can, how to make sense of a ballot on election day. We can travel alone. This is all new, and for some of us, it has not been easy. We were not raised to be independent, yet we have become so. We were not raised to live as single persons, yet we have found we can do so. We were not expected to take care of ourselves, yet we can, and we do. We have learned to value our own competence. Most of us still need and want a significant other in our lives, as partner, as companion, as lover, but we no longer need men to intercede for us with the outside world or tell us what to think.

> *My sister, when she turned fifty-three, it was awful. I couldn't believe it. She was a wreck. She sobbed and sobbed. And I'm thinking, at least she's married, she has a husband, she has a great life.*
> —Maureen

From my vantage point in a (seemingly) secure relationship that's closing in on thirty years, I know as little about what it's like to be single as I do about what it's like to be old. But most of my friends have been divorced at least once; several are still single (or single again). Margo's cousin Bette, who was also in a (seemingly) secure long-term relationship, is now a widow. Even when my marriage feels unsatisfactory and oppressive, as all marriages sometimes do, I would prefer to be in a relationship. But that's not because I'm afraid of being on my own, or even of being alone. I have friends, and I think I have the skills to make new ones. I am resourceful. I enjoy my own company, most of the time, and as I get older I am learning to appreciate the benefits of solitude.

> I can't get over this feeling that I really want a relationship. I know we're supposed to feel that we're complete, and all that. But I know I want that. It can't be your children. It can't be a girlfriend. It has to be a man. But you see some guy who looks neat, he's probably in his thirties. Maybe forties. But, hey, you look in the mirror and that's not what you are.
>
> —Melva

I watch Bette struggle with her newly acquired widowhood and wonder how I would manage in her place. Part of me thinks that if something should happen to my husband (God forbid), or if we ever decide to call it quits, I would not be eager to form a new relationship—it seems like an awful lot of work, learning to live with someone. But it would be arrogant and short-sighted of me to predict how I would handle the single life. My single friends run the gamut: Those who have never been in a long-term relationship and are quite content; those who have married and divorced several times trying to find true happiness; those who have suddenly noticed that they're getting older, and they're alone, and their choices have narrowed considerably; those who have married in their forties and fifties after being single for all or most of their lives.

> There's a part of me that says, "God, if I'm going to be alone, maybe I should be alone right now, while I've got resources and strength and independence." Not twenty years from now. How hard it will be. The fear of being a widow.
>
> —Vivian

Given the differences in life expectancy between men and women, most women can look forward to being single at some point in their lives. I agree with Vivian: It will be much harder later than it would be now. At least we can prepare, a little. We can make sure to retain a circle of friends. We can involve ourselves in activities outside the home. We can practice doing things on our own that we usually do with our partner. As I write, for example, Margo is in Paris, where she is ostensibly gathering information for a book but is mostly practicing being on her own. I do that occasionally (not in Paris, unfortunately); on business trips I spend my leisure time alone. I'm relatively comfortable eating in restaurants without a companion; I've learned to enjoy going to movies and visiting museums and taking walks by myself. I've also learned to appreciate being alone at home when my husband is away. It's not the same as being alone or on my own forever. But it is good practice.

> I'm so glad I'm single at fifty. I don't think about getting married again. I wouldn't say forever, because you never know, but I would have to have a lot of freedom. I've reached a point I think where I could be my own person. But five years ago, I couldn't be. I would become the other person. I would live for the other person. I think a lot of women do that. I have girlfriends who are single and fifty, and they can't wait to get married. And I think they are not whole people. They need somebody to be complete. And that's sad. If I did marry again, I'll never wear a ring, never. When I got married before, I wanted people to see my ring.
> —Maureen

> Marriage has never been a goal of mine. I like my solitude quite a bit.
> —Lynn

It can be good to have a partner, or at least a close companion, someone with whom you can share the morning newspaper over coffee, review the day over an evening meal, snuggle up to in bed. Someone to give you a neck rub or bring you chicken soup when you're sick. Someone with whom you can be yourself, someone you can be with for hours without speaking. But relationships are more fulfilling when both parties feel that they are together out of choice. And for some women, at some times, it has become possible for that choice to be remaining single.

RECONFIGURING THE FAMILY

THE EMPTY NEST

My children are growing up. My oldest went to the doctor, and when I called for an explanation of her condition, they said, "Sorry, we can't give out information without her permission." They took away my mother powers, without my even knowing it. And there's another side to that, which is, "What a relief."
                                                    —*Susan*

My mothering years started coming to an end when my son turned twelve. One morning, after he had spent the night with a friend, I ran into the two of them at the drugstore. With a big, "Hi, honey!" I reached for Aaron, to give him a hug. He pulled away as if my hands had burned his shoulders. We stood in the aisle next to the plastic dishpans talking awkwardly. "Did you have a good time?" I asked. "When will you be home?"

"Yeah, uh, I dunno," Aaron muttered, his eyes darting around to see who might be watching, then, "See ya," and he was off.

"Boy children," I said to no one in particular, and kept on with my shopping, trying to shrug off the disappointment and hurt. My youngest child was pushing me away, and I wasn't ready to let him go. My family was changing, and I wasn't sure it was a change I welcomed. But like so many life changes, it was one over which I had not the slightest control.

From my journal, four years later:

At sixteen, my youngest child backs away. His sister gone, he seeks his place in the family. We readjust. We're not

sure where he fits. He still spends some time with us,
talks guitar with Dad, reviews Spanish verbs with me. But
mostly he stays in his room where he has almost every-
thing he needs: a phone, a TV, a bed, his clothes.

But he's not quite ready to give us up. "What time will you
be home? You won't be late, will you? Call when the play is
over." And last night he came to my room where I lay
dozing over my book, and he leaned down, and he kissed
me goodnight.

I have just bought this same boychild a suit for his college
graduation. His sister, who is the age I was when her father and I
met, has set up housekeeping with her boyfriend and is working at
her first real job—one with benefits. My children have grown ten-
der toward me. Their hugs are now the gentle, reassuring hugs an
adult gives an older parent, not the fierce, clingy hugs I used to
get when they were little. Those are the hugs I miss, the "I love
you, Mom!" hugs, the cuddles, the giggles, the quiet moments over
Winnie the Pooh or *Wild Things* at bedtime. I miss the fun of revealing something new about the world to warm little beings who
believe that everything I say is right. I miss being the center of a
bright little creature's universe.

Don't get me wrong. This new situation is not bad, not at
all. My babies have been gone for a long time, and even though I
miss them, I like the adults they are becoming, these (almost)
grownups whose lives are increasingly peripheral to mine. In fact,
I like them more and more every year, as they continue to shed
their childish skins. I look with wonder on people who start new
families in midlife. I can understand the attraction of having a
loving infant to cuddle; I can appreciate the joys of watching a
child learn and grow. But I like my rediscovered independence,

and I wouldn't want to focus my diminishing energy on a child's tremendous needs. And I certainly wouldn't want to repeat the teenage years. Those years are much too hard, on the kids as well as on the parents. Almost-adults are too intense. They try too hard and want too much too fast. It's impossible to relax around them. Besides, they argue with you all the time.

> I got a lot of pleasure seeing the kids get mature, independent. That was a great relief, not having little kids around. I don't know how I survived all those years changing diapers and bundling them off in the morning. The empty nest is definitely part of the aging process. But it doesn't bother either of us at all. People always assume it will.
>
> —Anita

I have never regretted my decision to have children. For one thing, raising them has been a wonderful adventure; for another, I can see that intimate family connections will be increasingly important as I get older. I'm sure that the years when the children leave are far more difficult for women who define themselves primarily as "Mother," as well as for single mothers, especially those who have not prepared themselves, but I find more to like than to dislike about their going. I always knew they'd leave one day—that's what they're supposed to do, if you've done your job right. (All right, so it hasn't happened completely. So they've left half their stuff here. So they still got angry when we mentioned we were thinking of going to Oaxaca for Christmas without them. We're still in transition. But one day they *will* be gone for good—won't they?)

All in all, my empty nest feels like an opportunity, a chance to begin a new kind of life. The real problem these days is not how to fill the empty nest, but how to *keep* it empty. I hear that a lot of grownup (pardon me, "adult") children are coming back—sometimes with their own children—because they've lost a job or a spouse or want a break from independent living. What can you do? They're your kids—you have to take them in. And of course you want to help, even if it wreaks havoc with the new life you've been so carefully building.

> I feel as if my kids are my best friends. And when they do leave—although for years I thought, eighteen and out, can't wait, I see now that it really is like all those articles in Ladies' Home Journal. Leaving the nest, leaving the mom in the nest. That's another reason why during the next few months I want to prepare myself with some changes, some things to anticipate.
>
> —Lynn

By his last year of high school, Aaron tolerated our interference in his affairs only because we still controlled the money and the larder. (And, I'd like to think, because he was still unsure and needed us a little.) Jennifer came home from her junior year in Europe making all her own decisions and most of her own money. After two postgraduate years teaching in China, she rations our time with her. She sometimes asks for advice and even listens patiently to the unsolicited words of wisdom that drop without warning from our lips—but she does what *she* thinks best. We have been cut loose, relieved of—and stripped of—our parental powers *and* responsibilities. It's been years since we've had to consider kids when planning a meal, an evening out, or a vacation. We need think only of ourselves and the dog. It's a big change. After twenty-six years, we're not (primarily) Mommy and Daddy any more. The children are no longer connected by an umbilical cord but by a long elastic cord that sometimes snaps back with a jolt. In time, that cord will lose its elasticity and go slack. I find it both painful and wonderful that we are no longer central to our children's lives, that they no longer depend on us for their physical or psychological survival, that to them, we are moving from foreground to background. We're through (sort of); we've done our jobs, and if we've done them at all right and everyone has a little luck, our kids can manage their own lives. I hope we will remain close. I hope we will be able to help them out with money and advice and support when they need it. I hope they will want to spend time with us, not because they feel they must, but because they enjoy our company. I hope we will be friends.

I didn't start thinking about the future until the children were ready to leave.
— *Lynn*

My parents never made plans for what they'd do when my brother and I grew up and left. They just kept on living the way they had always lived, kept on with their lives in pretty much the same way, and now that they are in their eighties they still focus a lot of energy on trying to tell me, their fifty-year-old daughter, how to live her life. I am not going to do that. I am going to make plans, now, for the way to live the rest of my life.
— *Susan*

When I was pregnant, people were more than generous with advice about raising kids, and some of that advice was useful. Maybe a little advice would also be helpful when the kids are about to leave. For example, it's a good idea to begin developing your interests when the kids start high school. Unlike the endless years of elementary school, the high school years pass in a flash; when you've been busy taking care of other people and then you're not, free time can seem like empty time. A strong circle of friends takes on more importance when the nest empties; that's especially true for single parents. For couples, learning to spend time alone together while the kids are still around might reduce tensions when it's just the two of you at the dinner table, night after night.

Then there's the house. As soon as Jennifer left for China, I transformed her room into the home office I'd always wanted. Before Aaron left for college, I made him clean out his room, discard outgrown toys, pack up his Millennium Falcon and baseball cards. Of course, it was still his room for vacations and holidays. But now that he's graduating from the parental dole, we plan to tear the room down to the walls and transform it into a guest room/den/exercise room ... a grown-up sort of place. The kids will always be welcome—but it's our space now.

So that's one option: remodel. Take down the fading posters and grungy bulletin boards, paint the walls a color *you* like, replace the flimsy student desk and narrow bed with a sofabed and computer workstation, install bookshelves, and set up a Nordic Track. Create a new place in which you can welcome your adult children as guests, not as former residents, a place in which you can develop a new grownup relationship with them when they come to visit. A place in which you can get right on with your new life when they leave again.

The other option is to move. (*Of course* we'd leave a forwarding address.) When the kids come back, they come back to a different house, a grownup house, where they won't find forgotten kindergarten drawings tacked up in the den or outgrown sneakers wedged into corners of the closet or Bert and Ernie cups peering out from behind the good china. Moving might also be a good way to way to deal with those lingering feelings that the house is too empty, that it's missing part of itself, missing the family that made it a home.

From my journal, the week Aaron left for college:

> Last week I drove my youngest child and a carload of his worldly possessions to Southern California and abandoned him in a 10x12 concrete block room with two single beds, two small closets, two dressers, two desks, a bookshelf, and an eighteen-year-old boy he had never met. When I arrived home, my husband remarked, "This is an empty house." I looked around at the scattered cardboard boxes, single socks, fading Rams poster, tattered Teddy Bear, dusty Nintendo, and was too exhausted to weep. Was I sad? I would be sad. But I expected his footsteps on the deck. I expected the phone to ring: "I won't be home tonight, anyone call for me?" I expected the assault of hair spray in the bathroom, the toilet seat up, the unwashed juice bottle on the drainboard, the missing glasses and towels in his room.

> It's only been a week. This morning, the house did feel a little empty. I will be sad. Soon.

From Simone de Beauvoir:

> Here we come upon the sorry tragedy of the aged woman: she realizes she is useless; all her life the middle-class woman has often had to solve the ridiculous problem of how to kill time. But when the children are grown, the husband a made man or at least settled down, the time must still be killed somehow … with the needle or the crochet-hook, woman sadly weaves the very nothingness of her days. Watercolors, music, reading serve in much the same way; the unoccupied woman, in applying herself to such matters, is not trying to extend her grasp on

the world, but only to relieve her boredom. (Simone de Beauvoir, *The Second Sex*)

Simone de Beauvoir's description of the aging woman's fate chills me to the core of my being. She could have been writing about *me*, about the life I should have had. Luckily, that's not the life I'm having. Killing time is the least of my concerns. By the time the kids left, I was ready—even impatient—to shed the parenting role, to get on with my own life and let the kids get on with theirs. Unlike my grandmothers, I can realistically look forward to two or three more decades of active life. Unlike my grandmothers and mother, I have a life apart from my role as wife and mother. I have my work. I enjoy taking classes, becoming involved in new projects. I have no trouble filling up my days.

Nevertheless, the childless life is an adjustment. The house did seem empty for a time when our family was reduced from four to three. When Aaron left, and we were only two, I found myself feeling my way through a new silence, trying to breathe quietly and deliberately into a vast new empty space in my life. Four years later, odd feelings descend without warning and startle me, like turning to find that a stranger has silently entered the room while my back was turned. One night I dreamed we had a third child, a twelve-year-old girl named Sarah who had gone off on vacation with a friend's family and who we had completely forgotten. I felt devastated. I felt tremendous guilt: How could you lose your own child? At the same time I felt tremendous resentment: I didn't want to have discovered Sarah. I didn't want another child in my life.

It seems that I've entered another of those definable life stages of life, the stage of childless parent. Sometimes I long for the beautiful babies who gaze at me from picture frames all over the house.

But then I remember that my babies are not missing, only transformed. We have a new and different relationship, and we are embarking on new—and different—journeys. They are beginning their own life adventures, and now I have the time and space to begin a great new adventure of my own.

CHANGING FAMILIES

Every single one of my mother's sisters' children, without exception, is divorced.
                                        —*Vivian*

For my parents' fiftieth wedding anniversary, my brother and I threw a party to celebrate the event and honor them in the way they honored their parents when I was a teenager and more interested in meeting cute cousins than in considering what my grandparents' long lives together meant. My parents' party was the first time in forever that all my aunts and uncles and cousins and cousins' spouses and cousins' children had been in the same place at the same time. After dinner, while my brother spoke a few words to thank our parents for being wonderful parents, I gazed at all those familiar faces and realized that of our generation, only my brother and I and three cousins on my mother's side (two of whom are older than I am) were still married to our original spouses. Yet in my parents' generation, all but one aunt and one uncle remained married to their original partners until death did them part.

In my parents' generation, people got married and stayed that way, all my aunts and uncles. And of my mother's four children, we're all four divorced. And that hurts her.
                                        —*Melva*

At a dinner party, we discover that all four couples at the table are in long-term relationships. We are amazed. It's rare today, at least here on the West Coast, for people to stay married until they reach middle age. For better or worse, many of my children's friends grew up in a new sort of "extended family" that in some odd ways resembles the extended families of our parents' youth: Lots of relatives, lots of presents for birthdays and graduations, lots of people to invite to weddings.

But this new extended family is different. It's no longer mom, dad and the kiddies and four grandparents and ten or twelve aunts and uncles, but mom (usually) and the kiddies, and then (often), mom and the kiddies, and dad and his new partner and the kiddies, and then the new kiddies, and then mom and dad his new wife and her kiddies and mom's new partner and his kiddies and their kiddies and grandma and grandpa and grandma and grandpa and the new grandma and grandpa who are mom and dad's new wife's and mom's new husband's mom and dad, and everyone's brothers and sisters who have become new uncles and aunts and cousins.

Six years ago, I commiserated with a close friend who had divorced her first husband when their three children were under the age of twelve, then remarried and had a fourth child with her new husband. My friend was anxious about complex familial relationships that threatened to ruin her oldest daughter's college graduation. She and her husband could hardly say a civil word to one another even after ten years apart. Her new husband didn't particularly want to meet her first husband. The prospect of her daughter's maternal grandmother, paternal grandmother, stepgrandmother, stepgrandfather, father's sister, mother's brother, stepfather's sister, brother, sister, stepbrother, and assorted cousins all together in the same place gave her a stomach ache.

I hear that the graduation went relatively smoothly. A glutton for punishment, however, my friend is getting ready to repeat the process for her daughter's wedding; in the meantime, her daughter's father has divorced his second wife and has a new lady friend.

I really have to think hard to think of friends and family members who aren't divorced, and when I think of someone, I realize it's usually a second marriage.

—*Vivian*

It has to be awfully confusing for the kids. How do they keep track of everyone when the cast of characters keeps changing? Between dawn and dusk, a child can lose or gain a parent, get a new set of siblings and new grandparents, aunts, uncles, and cousins. With each divorce and remarriage a child's position in the family can change abruptly—Johnny, the baby, now has two younger sisters; Cindy, the eldest (and her father's pet) is now a middle child. Wendy lives alone with her mother in a small apartment, but she is the youngest of three when she stays with her father and stepmother in their big house in Beverly Hills. Jason is an only child most of the year when he lives with his dad and his dad's lover in Seattle, but he's the big brother when he spends summers in Maine with his mother, her new husband, and their new baby. It's no wonder that "The Brady Bunch" was so popular with our kids that they memorized entire episodes.

This redefinition of the American family started in my parents' generation, when divorce became possible, not desirable, not frequent, but possible, because women were being educated, could find jobs, didn't always go right from Daddy's house to marriage so they had some experience of the world, and even though their choices were limited, could take care of themselves if they had to. Divorce became an option if a husband was abusive or played around too much or was a poor provider. But it meant failure, and it was a last resort. Our generation, however, has raised divorce to an art form. It's become almost routine for people to split up if things are going badly, if they feel they have made a mistake, if the marriage has run out of steam. If they're not happy. If they want something more. Why not? After all, Fritz Perls was one of our gurus.

Some experts say that we're in transition from one type of family structure to another—that the Ozzie and Harriet/Donna Reed/Beaver Cleaver model is so unworkable that we must find alternatives. That might be true. We live in a complicated and rapidly changing world; we need more flexible, more workable family structures. There's nothing intrinsically right about the way that two-parent father-mother nuclear families raise kids. As long as the basic family values are there, as long as the people doing the child-raising provide the love and caring and security and stability and support and guidance children need, it doesn't matter whether there are a mother and father, or two mothers, or two fathers, or one mother or one father, or a household full of people.

My friends and I are pretty much done with our child-raising. We've made our choices, and our kids have had to live with them. And we have created a few new models for our younger siblings and our children. We've raised the possibility of making choices, of experimenting with lifestyles. I hope that younger parents are able to learn from our sometimes unsuccessful attempts to find workable and satisfying ways to raise our children. I hope they will remember that children don't have much say in their parents' choices, and that parents must be responsible for considering their children's needs along with their own. I hope they make choices that enable their children to grow up healthy and able to raise strong, healthy families of their own.

HARD TIMES

IT'S ABOUT TIME

One of the most amazing things is the passage of time. It's astonishing to me. Scary. My mother has told me it increases. Forties are fast, fifties are faster, sixties still faster, seventies you wouldn't even believe.

—Vivian

"Time is short, too short," my mother's youngest sister says sadly at my parents' fiftieth anniversary party. I agree. There isn't enough time. It's like being at a birthday party when you're a kid. You're waiting for your turn at Pin the Tail on the Donkey and then it's going to be Musical Chairs and you're good at that. You glance at the clock, good, almost an hour left, and then, wham! There's Mom, "Time to go, sweetie."

"But I'm not ready yet," you whimper.

"Sorry, honey, I left a pot on the stove." The other kids get to stay, but you have to leave before you had a chance to play this great game.

So I'm oversimplifying. Life is not a birthday party. But it is going to be over all too soon, far sooner than I ever thought possible. I don't want to waste my precious time looking at the clock. I want to make the best use of it I can.

I want to put my pawprint on something. Somehow, we've saved that up. The generation behind us wanted to be famous when they were twenty, and we've waited until we were in our fifties and sixties even to begin to think about such a thing.

—Susan

One of the big differences about being in my fifties is the feeling that, okay, if I'm going to write fiction, I'd better damn well better just write it. Because I don't have that much time left. I can't bullshit around about it. How long will I have? Will I reach seventy-five like my aunt? At what age will I die? The sense of time is starting to motivate me a little bit. I promised myself to retire when I'm sixty. I can become an emeritus professor if I want. But the other thing I'm seriously thinking about is becoming a judge. I like robes, and people stand up when you come in, and you get in the middle of everybody's business.

—Betty

Among other things, getting old means losing your future, that endless future you used to have, that infinite stretch of time in which you could do anything you wanted to do: Build a career, make a fortune, build your dream house, travel, do good works, learn to ski, run for Congress, win a Pulitzer, study the classics, write poetry .... You have that stretch of time until the last day of your forty-ninth year. Then it's gone, forever. You can see the end coming up fast. You realize that you'd better start making choices. You'd better decide what's important.

I shift my point of view and see the whole thing differently. I see an interesting paradox: Now that my time is limited, time means less to me than it ever did. It's not nearly as worrisome. Even though I sometimes experience a sudden, strong need to *do it now!*, I no longer feel much urgency. I no longer have to rush, to get it all in, the way I did when I was young. I watch with interest (and an ache in the pit of my stomach) as my children struggle with their need for everything to happen *now!* Next month, next year, next decade still has little reality for them. I was like that yesterday, anxious, impatient, grasping, scared. When did that change? Why is it that with fewer years ahead, I see more possibilities. They may be more limited, but they are far more attainable.

I am finally starting to believe that one does have a finite amount of time left to live, and I see that there are many things about life that I like better than all the things about life I haven't liked, and that I really value it, and it's really precious, and the quality of my time I want to be spent in the best possible ways. That's my duty to myself. To support myself in a more pleasing way and to cherish my time. Now, to sit on a deck and watch the light change in a certain way would be completely amusing, fascinating.

—Lynn

Around my fortieth birthday I started doing things for myself, being nicer to myself. That's when I first started getting facials and going to residential spas and exercising. I'd never done those sorts of things before. It was the first realization that things are finite, and I wanted to do things now that I would enjoy, because you can't save them for your next lifetime.

—Anita

My friend Linda Mukai died, after a two-and-a-half-year struggle with colon cancer. Never during that two and a half years was her life expectancy more than six months. Linda was a true Type A person who worked long hours at her successful consulting business and still found time for her son and husband. The most well-organized person I knew, she carried a thick Dayrunner in which she scheduled every minute of her life. Unlike most Type A people I've known, however, Linda never appeared intense or driven; she was almost always bright and cheerful, with a clear, focused energy that made her easy and fun to work with. That's why I was so surprised to learn, several months after her cancer was diagnosed, that the year before, she was so depressed that she had started seeing both a psychiatrist and a psychologist.

Immediately after the cancer diagnosis, when she was given her first "six months to live," Linda began reordering her priorities to make time for what she considered important: her family and her friends. She began closing down her business. She decorated her living room and landscaped her back yard, which she had put off since she and her husband, Craig, had moved into their new house several years earlier. She spent unstructured time with her son, Matt. She and Craig took trips to Arizona and Hawaii and Palm Springs. A year after the diagnosis, when she was weak and ill from the chemotherapy, she and Craig threw a huge party, bringing together more than one hundred people she cared about, friends, business associates and family members. Before she died, she told me that the first year of her illness had been the happiest year of her life.

> *Lately time is stretching out and shortening. It keeps playing tricks, and I keep playing with it.*
>
> —Margo

Not much is certain in this life. All we know for sure is that we will die some day, and that time passes. But while the moment of death is somewhat definable, it's more difficult to characterize the passage of time. It can pass in a flash, or it can seem not to move at all. It can feel rich and full, or empty and unsatisfying. Each moment can be experienced as impatience for the next, or longing for what's gone before—or it can simply be experienced. But it seems to me that if you can learn to live in the now ... now

… now … now, instead of in the when … when … when … when … then the moment in which time stops for you will be another moment, another of the millions of experiences that are the sum of your life.

I hear … the hum of my computer, the rush of rainwater down the drain outside the window, the click click click of the computer keys, the soft rush of air in and out of my body with each inhale and exhale …

I see … bare branches silhouetted against gray clouds, rain-drops falling from the eaves, papers scattered on my desk, a glass mug with an inch of cold coffee at the bottom, a black and white photo of my daughter at age two, intent on digging in a chipped flower pot …

I smell … the dry odor of dust, the slightly acrid odor from the furnace …

I taste … bitter coffee on my tongue …

I touch … smooth plastic, rough skin, tangled hair, soft lips …

I feel … my back supported by a soft cushion, glasses resting on my nose, the expanding and contraction of my rib cage with each inhalation and exhalation …

I think there's a choice you make when you realize your mortality, and that can be at thirty, or fifty, or eighty, the choice of whether to jump in and do it, or to mark time. Our mothers were always marking time, from the time their babies left the house. When you get right down to it, what are we all doing but marking time? And we make that time count, we can make it productive, we can make it fun. Who are we bullshitting? Is winning an Academy Award important? It's marking time. Is it more fun than shopping at Loehmann's?

—Leslie

*It's going to take me about ten years to get a B.A. That's
okay with me. There's a woman about eighty-eight years
old at the College of Marin, doing math.*

—*Maureen*

What I try to keep in mind about time is that it doesn't really matter. I can't control its passing, so why worry? I *can* control
the way I choose to use it, to experience it. I can choose to be
aware, make conscious choices, live in the moment as often as I
can, decide what's important and get rid of or ignore what's not. I
used to think that making the best use of my time meant keeping
busy at tasks, or if I wasn't doing tasks, working at my relationships, or if I wasn't doing that, reading, or if I wasn't doing that,
taking a brisk walk to get my heart rate up. Being "productive."
Now I'm discovering that the best use of my time is simply doing
whatever it is I'm doing, even if that is sitting quietly watching a
fly buzz around the room.

Developing the ability just to be, to experience the moment
as life itself, may be the magic that allows a person to retain the
pleasure of life into old age. As my parents' activities have become more and more circumscribed, I've noticed that staving off
boredom is one of the most difficult aspects of getting old. My
father has always been an active person. Now he is so ill with
heart disease that he can do little more than sit and watch television all day. I am also an active person; what will I do with myself
when my body slows to the point where I can no longer keep
"busy"? When I can no longer be "productive"? I'm terrified by
the prospect of spending my declining years in front of a television set, day upon tedious day. I want, instead, to learn how to see
and experience ordinary everyday moments with new eyes, to be
able to capture at will the wonder that I sometimes feel at the first

taste of morning coffee, the crisp touch of chill air on a foggy morning, the soft caress of a worn bathrobe against my thigh. The best use of my time might be to write a page, clean out a closet, have lunch with a friend, or take an acting class. It might be to sit in a Paris cafe sipping a café crème and watching people come and go, or walk down a street I've walked a thousand times feeling the warm sun on my back, or lie in a warm bath recalling how it felt to sit in a rocking chair at 2 A.M. nursing my firstborn child. It might be putting my work aside and watching out the window while the sky changes color from gray to blue and back again, which is what I am going to do right now.

ON BEING OLD

My biggest concern is my health. I think it would be so hard to be alive and not have your faculties and your health, not to be able to be on your own. To be in pain.

—Melva

My father, who has congestive heart disease, spent much of this spring in the hospital undergoing various procedures, hooked up to machines, getting better, getting worse, and getting better again. Surgery is out of the question. All the doctors can do is try to find the right balance of drugs to keep his heart from failing. Despite the odds, he has made it home. He appears to be recovering, but for a man his age with his poor health, "recovery" is a relative term. Recovery means only that he's not dead and is somewhat able to take care of himself. He will never again be healthy. He will never again play golf or do much work in his garden. His traveling days are over; even if he felt well enough, my mother would never agree because she panics at the thought of being more than a few miles from his doctors. At best, he will be a semi-invalid whose heart might fail again at any moment. This is considered a good prognosis. "After all," the doctor says, "he is an eighty-year-old man."

"Eighty?" I think. "But eighty's not so old."

The physical hindrances are of course important, no matter how little an old person manages to admit their dominance. As I write this I am well into my seventies, and I think that I have aged faster than I meant to ... (I resent

being stiff and full of creaks and twinges). I wish all of us could prepare ourselves for [the dismays and delights of old age] as instinctively and with as much outside help as we do those of puberty, adolescence, pregnancy ...
(M. F. K. Fisher, *Sister Age*)

I hate seeing my father's decline. It makes me terribly sad. And mingled with my concern for him, and for my mom, is concern for myself. Getting old is scary. It's coming up so fast, and I'm not ready. Not ready for my body to deteriorate, that's for sure, and not ready in other ways as well. For one thing, I don't have nearly enough money.

What happens when you get old, without money, without insurance—do you become a bag lady? I'm afraid that nobody will care, nobody will know.
—Susan

One of my fears is being eighty or ninety and having no money and no one to care for me. My mother used to throw that in my face: "If you don't have kids, who's going to take care of you?" What's interesting is that I've begun to understand my mother's thinking, her fears.
—Sachiko

At a dinner party, much talk about retirement. We've talked about retiring since we were twenty-five, but always with a laugh: "When we make our millions, man, we'll retire!" The laughs are shakier these days. Our children are gone or on their way out. Our bodies are slowing down and every day brings new aches and pains. Our parents are becoming infirm and starting to die. Every few months someone our own age is diagnosed with cancer or has an unexpected heart attack. We're not old, yet, but we are certainly older, and it's no longer possible to deny that we are going to be old *tomorrow*, not in some distant future, but *tomorrow*. We're getting worried: "Will we have enough money? Thank God we own a house. Have you looked into nursing home insurance?" We're making tentative plans: "A bookstore might be nice. Is there an age limit for Peace Corps volunteers?" In the middle of the night, I run figures in my head, calculating how much we're going to need to get by. And I want more than to get by. I want more than to stay off the streets. I want comfort. I want the freedom to travel and go to the theater and eat at good restaurants. I want my own tennis court, damn it, and there isn't enough time to amass the fortune I'm surely going to need. My husband's way of dealing with this concern is to buy lottery tickets that he crumples with a curse when he doesn't win. I scoff, but I'm also playing the lottery, going about my life as if the money we'll need is just around the corner, nursing the fantasy that my husband will write a best-selling novel that becomes a blockbuster film or my business will be bought out by a multinational concern. We might as well go to Reno and wager our retirement fund on the craps tables.

From my journal:

> Sometimes I feel like a locomotive chug-chugging toward the top of the hill, and it seems like a long way off, except it's not, and one of these days I'll reach the top and then find myself speeding down the other side. And I don't think I'm going to be ready.

When I consider how little planning we've done for our "golden" years, I wonder where we got this cockiness, this arrogance, this blind confidence that everything will work itself out so why worry? Was it because we were raised in the happy-go-lucky Fifties when Americans honestly believed that each generation would be better off economically than the one before? Because we became hippies in the Sixties when it was uncool to worry about money? Or because we are an unusually fortunate generation with almost unlimited opportunities who have never had to worry much about security? Compared to the generations before and after us, everything came easily for us. If you were smart, you could easily get into the college of your choice, and if your family didn't have much money, excellent public education was readily available. Jobs were plentiful. One person's salary was enough to support a family. You could buy a house for only a few thousand dollars down, and low interest rates and property taxes kept mortgage payments affordable. Medical care was reasonably priced. We saw no reason to worry about the future. We lived from day to day, not bothering to look too far ahead. How naive we were! But who could imagine that by the Eighties, it would take a fortune to put a kid through college? That by the Nineties even a graduate degree would be no guarantee of a stable, well-paying job? That an ordinary house could cost a quarter of a million dollars, or losing a job could mean losing health insurance, which in turn could mean that a serious illness could lead to bankruptcy? That pension funds could go broke and Social Security might run out of money just when we need it? That the kids would come home again or need help coming up with a down payment or staying current with a student loan, and we would have to break into our nest eggs again and again, helplessly, as a tiny voice murmured warnings.

And that commune in the country I once envisioned as the refuge of my old age doesn't seem nearly as appealing now.

I must be the only person in Marin whose stocks went down and whose house hasn't appreciated in value. I should be doing better.

—Overheard in a cafe

I eavesdrop as the women at the next table talk intently over their lattés. The younger one looks out of place here in her tan slacks and ivory silk blouse; then I understand that this is a business meeting, that she is here to sell something to the older woman in the jogging suit and tennis shoes that are now *de rigueur* for an afternoon coffee with friends or meetings with financial planners. The older woman, whose auburn hair is too dark to be natural, shuffles papers and waits anxiously for reassurance that she's doing fine, that she's just like everyone else even though everyone else is driving a BMW and she's nursing along a tired '86 Volvo station wagon she can barely afford to insure. She is fifty-three or fifty-four and terrified that she will be poor. As retirement looms, she has discovered that the tiny percentage of her salary she will receive after thirty-five years of teaching might not cover her bills. She is looking for magic, a wishing well, a fairy godmother: Tap, tap, here you are my dear, a pot of gold to smooth the way.

I listen, and I think about my fears, dark creatures sitting quietly at the back of my mind, mostly unnoticed, mostly ignored. It's only on bad days, when I'm tired, sick, pre-menstrual (or menopausal), that they rise up to take stage, terrifying in their dense unyielding blackness. My fears have names, although I hesitate to speak them for fear of raising devils. So I'll name them softly:

Losing my health

Losing my parents

Losing my husband

Losing a child

Being old, sick and poor, alone and lonely

Suffering a long painful illness

Becoming senile

Losing control of my body

I notice that my own death is not on the list, and I realize that death is not among my greatest fears. I am far more concerned about what is to come between now and the moment of my death than I am with the event itself.

Getting older terrifies me, the thought of my own mortality, because I'm still in the phase of my life where I think I can live forever. I have not accepted the fact that I'm going to have to die someday.

—Judy

It's closer to the end. You've probably passed the halfway point, because you know you probably won't live to be a hundred, and if you did, what condition would you be in?

—Melva

It's not the number of years we have left that interests us, it's the number of good years: How long will we feel good, be sexy, be able to play tennis, hike, work, travel? Consciously or unconsciously we've divided the rest of our lives into "good" years and "bad" years. The bad years, I suppose, will be the ones when we will be *really* old. When we are sick. When we are frail. When we are incapacitated. As I write the words I feel a chill. How can that happen to me? Must that happen to me? And how many more "good" years will I have? Twenty? Twenty-five? Will I be able to play tennis at eighty-five? There is so much I want to do.

So much of my energy has gone into defying limitations. I
don't stop if I have a cold, if I'm exhausted. But now we're
talking about approaching something we can't ignore.

—*Vivian*

Much of this speculation is an exercise in futility. Not the money part; that's real, and it needs attention *now*. But I am looking at old age from the outside. Even though I concede that I am mortal and, yes, my lifespan is limited, and yes, I will get old *someday*. I am no more able to conceive of myself as seventy or eighty or ninety than my daughter and her friends can conceive of being fifty-five. I can assume that there will be bad days and good days, just as in any stage of life. And I can prepare. The money is only part of it. What's just as important is learning to *live*. To hone my senses and experience my life instead of drifting through. That means slowing down. Watching and listening and tasting my life. Taking advantage of opportunities to try something new. Reordering priorities, as my friend Linda did when she knew that she was dying. Taking the time to practice living for and in the moment. Because in the end, that's all we really have: Now, and now, and now, and now.

MORTALITY AND LOSS

In these last two years I have had to witness too much decline … Perhaps I cried so much because Scrabble [her old cat] had become a symbol of … the breakup about which we are helpless, which we have to witness in others, and in ourselves, year by year. How does one deal with it? (May Sarton, *The House by the Sea: A Journal*)

I have suddenly found myself face to face with people my age who are dying. Once you've turned fifty you know there is no such thing as immortality. I was immortal until this year. Immortality has to do with there was always going to be a tomorrow.

—Susan

The week my daughter returned from China I walked into the kitchen to find her weeping over her high school's alumni newspaper. "What's the matter?" I asked. She pointed to the photograph of a classmate who had been killed in a plane crash. He was twenty-five years old. "Twenty-five-year-old people are not supposed to die," I thought, and gave my daughter a long, hard hug, as if by holding her to me I could keep her safe.

I don't want to think about death and dying. Not my own so much, but losing people I care about. I don't like that, even though I know I have to do it. Sometimes I think that this is preparation for getting us through to the next time. I worry about Bob's mother. She keeps cleaning out her stuff and simplifying her life more and more. It's perfectly

*okay for me to dissolve into pure light, but I have no
interest in her or my mother doing it.*

—*Margo*

I was well into middle age before I lost anyone close to me.
except my grandparents, of course, but they were old (to me) and
no longer part of my everyday life. I felt sad and missed them, but
I was young and busy and quite able to shed my tears and go on
with my life. It's different now. The people in my parents' generation have started to die. Four years ago, my husband's father. Two
years ago, my mother's brother-in-law, my uncle Sid, followed only
a few months later by my aunt Dee. Last year, my father's brother-
in-law, my uncle Lee, and two of my husband's aunts. It's mortality looking me in the face that my father, who has always been so
vital, who has always intimidated the hell out of me, who I have
spent most of my life trying to impress, now needs me to take care
of him. After quadruple bypass surgery ten years ago, he began to
slow down. Now that he is failing, my mother, my brother, and I
must prepare ourselves to lose him.

The stress of my father's illness has exhausted my mother
who, at eighty, is still relatively healthy. I've noticed that she feels
light in my arms, as though she is starting to disappear. She's also
been hospitalized a couple of times, has had a cancer scare, nothing too serious, but a foreboding. Like so many of my friends, I am
struggling with the reality that my parents are going to die. No
matter how much I want to accept death as a natural part of life,
I'm not ready to give them up. I'm not grown up enough to be an
orphan. Not yet. Not ever.

*I have a fear I don't like to talk about, of my husband's
mortality. Seeing him age, my best and worst friend from
the age of nineteen, seeing him able to do less, not feel-*

ing well some of the time, gray hair, looser muscles. And realizing the possibility of losing him, and I would be an old lady alone. I think about it often. It's not that I couldn't live without him. I could do that. But I would miss this person. I really would miss this person tremendously.

—Vivian

It's not only old people who are getting sick and dying. A friend in his late fifties has a stroke while motoring through Europe; another friend, even younger, is forced by a heart attack to take early retirement. A man a year younger than me has an angioplasty. My friend Linda is only forty-eight when she loses her struggle with colon cancer. Another friend survives a heart attack in his mid-fifties, only to die from lung cancer a few years later. All around me women are losing their breasts to surgeons' knives, their hair to chemotherapy. My husband and one of our woman friends, both of whom have raised exercise to an art form, fight dangerously high levels of cholesterol. It's become clear that we can no longer fully trust in tomorrow. It would be foolish to put off what we really want to do.

There's also the big thing about getting closer to dying. Understanding profoundly to the tips of my toes that youth is gone and a lot of my life is gone, and there can certainly be some wonderful years, but inevitably there's going to be either sudden death or a painful illness, and loss of dear ones. Before, it was something that happened to somebody else. Oddly enough, it doesn't make me unhappy. It's going to be part of life. There's no therefore.

—Vivian

In today's science-fiction world, it's not completely out of the question that someone could accomplish the unimaginable:

Come up with a cure for death. Would such a "cure" be a great achievement? Humankind doesn't seem to be doing too well as it is, and immortality would undoubtedly cause some *serious* problems. But I wonder how different humans would be if we were not mortal, if we did not know that we were going to die someday. Can we even imagine immortality? Life in our universe exists in a cycle of birth, growth, maturity, aging, and death. Not dying would so substantially change what we are that the consequences of a "cure" for mortality are inconceivable. If we did not die, we would no longer be human. We would be God.

> *When you have friends die around you and they're your age ... suddenly I have this tremendous need for fun and fluff.*
>
> —Susan

> *I used to think of death, and I used to be afraid of it. I'm not any more.*
>
> —Maureen

I don't know that I've ever been afraid of death, per se. The process of dying perhaps, but not death itself. Maybe that's not entirely true. But my own death seems a long, long way off, and it's hard to hold onto a fear of something that doesn't seem immediate or real. I know people who believe that death is a passage into another, better life, and I imagine that such faith is a comfort. I hold no such belief, although I like to think that after my body dies my "soul," whatever that may be, will return to something larger and greater than myself. I'm not concerned about the moment of my dying. What does concern me is the process that leads up to that moment, a process that is likely to include some degree of pain, discomfort, helplessness, and humiliation. There's something to be said for going quickly, the way my husband's aunt Rose did when her heart suddenly gave out last year. It was a brutal shock for her family, but at least she didn't suffer a lingering illness. I hope that when my time comes, I can go quickly, without much bother. If it becomes necessary, I hope that someone will have the compassion to help me into that long goodnight when I say I'm ready. After all, maybe the most we can do for one another in this world is help each other into it, through it, and out of it with as much caring and compassion as we can muster.

When I let myself dwell on this subject (not often), I sometimes wonder why we must suffer before we die. Why must our bodies deteriorate? Why must we become weak and helpless? Wouldn't it be nice if we could keep our youth, our stamina, our beauty, our energy, our passion until the last moment and die quickly, before we are forced to suffer?

Suppose the angel were to come down and say, have it your way, I'll pluck you off in your prime. Would I be ready? Not likely. I'd feel too good. I wouldn't have a sense of closure, a sense that I'd lived out my cycle. I'd feel as if I were missing out. I wouldn't know, the way my friend Diane's ninety-two-year-old mother knew, that it was my time. I'd kick and scream all the way.

The price we pay for the gift of life is mortality. Eventually slowing down and dying, possibly being ill and uncomfortable along the way, is unalterably part of the experience of living. I hope to have many years of healthy life ahead; when the angel does come for me, I hope that I will feel the way Diane's mother felt, that I've lived out my cycle and am ready to go. For now, though, I see no point in dwelling on something over which I have little if any control. What's important now is to concern myself with what I can control, the rest of my life, the part that comes between now and the moment of my death. I have so much more to do.

THE TRUTH

ABOUT

MIDDLE AGE

MIDDLE AGE IS SO MUCH FUN!

The truth about fifty is simple. At long last, I can become the curmudgeon I have always wanted to be. I can make ugly faces at parents who bring their children to restaurants. I can say obnoxious things to strangers, I can swear in the supermarket and be ignored. I am revving up to be a feisty old bat.
—Susan

The big secret about middle age is that it can be so much fun. Not go-out-and-boogie-all-night fun (unless that's what turns you on), but a quieter, more subtle kind of fun, a chuckle here, a giggle there, a funny warm bubbly feeling in the pit of your stomach from a sudden awareness of nothing much at all. There's so much about myself I like now, so much about my life. I enjoy musing about the adventures still to come. I welcome the opportunities to learn something new, to strike out in new directions, to test myself. I love this new feeling that I no longer have to answer to anyone, to explain myself, to impress other people. After more than fifty years of life, I am finally free to be myself.

The thing I am enjoying the most is that for the first time in my life I am really who I am. I accept my own confusion, ambivalence, the fact that I'm complex. So on alternate Tuesdays I don't have a clue as to who I am. But the rest of the week I'm pretty clear.
—Susan

I like the wisdom, of course, a much better understanding of who I am, and what the world is about, how people work. I wouldn't want to give that up.

—Melva

A few years ago I belonged to a small writing group in which we read what we were working on and gave each other feedback. One evening a woman in her early thirties read a scene from her new play. It was good, and we told her so. She grinned and said, "I'm so happy to be writing!" She paused, then added, "Why did I wait so long to start doing this?" Another woman, close to my own age, replied, "You needed the life experience to write." And the first woman turned to the second and said, "Thank you."

The older I've gotten the better I feel about myself. I'm pretty clear about what I'm doing. My confidence is there, so I can go ahead and do it without a lot of other things getting in the way.

—Sachiko

It's really neat to have young people look up to you. I'm finally getting the recognition after all these years. I love to nurture younger women. It feels good when you give them the background they don't get from anyone else. It's a perk.

—Betty

One thing I love about being older is knowing more, and being better able to make more sense of what I know. It's wonderful to discover that you own a treasure trove of life experience and knowledge—it's like finding out that the tie-dyed T-shirts and Mouse posters you've been storing in the basement since the early Seventies have become valuable over the years. All that information I've gathered, all those seemingly unrelated skills I've learned, all the time and money I've spent to expand my self-awareness, all my successes and failures, the boring stuff, the fun stuff—they're gold! They all make me a fuller, richer, more complex, more knowledgeable, more complete person than I could possibly have been at twenty-five, or thirty, or forty-two. And not only have the treasures helped create the person I am today, they make possible the person I am to become.

> It's great to be old enough to be secure enough to really know what you want. You're comfortable with who you are. As you get older, the larger differences don't matter so much. I can do what I can do. I know it real well. Your identity gets clearer and clearer, and that feels real good. You don't spend a lot of time worrying, and if you don't wear the right thing, and you don't say the right thing, tough. It takes all the burden off of having to be perfect.
>
> —Leslie

> I think you can keep getting better. As long as you keep redefining what it is that you're trying to achieve. If I keep trying to run the Pacific Sun race faster every year, there's going to be some point where I can't. I will have peaked, and I'll only know it after I've done it. "Oh, yeah, back there in 1989, when I … " But if I keep trying to grow in my awareness of reality, and in my compassion for myself and for others, and maybe even wisdom, and maybe even the ability to listen and care, or maybe even to have pockets of peace and contentment, there should be no end to that. I should be able to grow, endlessly.
>
> —Vivian

Webster's defines wisdom as "the power of judging rightly

and following the soundest course of action, based on knowledge, experience, understanding, etc." That definition gives the cliché "older but wiser" a certain cachet. And once you get a little wisdom, you understand how precious it is. What a gift! You live long enough, you get wrinkles, you get aches and pains, you get paunchy, your eyes get bad—and *voilà*! In the door comes wisdom. You achieve something new, the ability to see things in context, to know what this means in relationship to that, to understand what's important and what's not, what's lasting and what's transitory. To have a new sense of where you fit in your universe. You won't like everything that comes with aging. Nobody welcomes physical deterioration and the loss of loved ones. But we didn't much like the pimples and peer pressure and anxieties that accompanied the discovery of sex and the endless energy of our teens and early twenties, either, or the sleepless nights and unending demands and constant worry that came with the adventure of parenthood, or the stress and conflicting expectations and uncertainties that went along with the excitement of building a career. We've got to accept the unpleasantries that come with aging in return for good stuff, the wisdom, the growth and learning, the continuing experience of becoming ... ourselves.

> *Something good about turning fifty, a certain scope of perception, a feeling that one finally does understand one's place in the universe, and one's self, and one's relationship to other people, and how much people can expect to do individually in their lives, and to accept oneself personally for what they are and they aren't. That's gratifying and relieving. And it does seem to take at least half a lifetime to achieve.*
>
> —Lynn

My nicest fiftieth birthday present was California Indian Educator of the Year. That came as a tremendous sense of relief. I used to feel insecure. I'm not feeling that way now. I'm beginning to feel my own voice, and my right to my own voice.

—Betty

Teaching is something I've always enjoyed, and I've never been a better teacher than I am today. It's more than knowing a lot about how people learn, and more than having amassed a lot of knowledge. I'm a better teacher now because I understand how what I teach relates to people's lives. I understand what's important. I can give my students a perspective rooted in decades of experience. I can voice my opinions with confidence, because I understand that being right is not what's important. I can present my point of view without needing to make people agree with me.

Turning fifty was great. If I had an opinion and some man didn't like it, tough!

—Overheard remark

I've learned that if they can walk around and act up, I can walk around and act up. If they can say in a meeting what they feel like saying, I can say what I feel like saying, and then I began to get feedback that showed they were listening! It was like I decided I had a right to breathe, I had a right to my opinion, and it was okay if someone felt offended or didn't agree with me. It took me years to do that.

—Melva

While putting together this book and talking with other women in their fifties, I notice that we keep making the point that it's okay to get older. Of course it's okay. The only other choice is unacceptable. It would be silly to deny that we are getting older, day by day, hour by hour, minute by minute; we need to accept reality, and move on.

What we may be trying to articulate is that there are things about getting older that are okay. Aging is not only about getting old, it's about everything that life is about: learning, experimenting, and growing; failing and succeeding; being pleased and disappointed; feeling sad one day and elated the next. Aging is part of the process of becoming oneself, a process that isn't over until it's over. Midlife is a stage in that process, a stage that, like all the others, brings something valuable we didn't have before.

> I like myself a lot, getting older. And I like everybody else a lot. The anger is gone, a lot of the angst is gone. The assholes will always be there, but it's such a relief not to give a damn one way or the other. There's such compassion. I feel like I'm getting younger, in a way.
>
> —Margo

> Being an Indian woman, the old ladies run everything. In the Indian community, people do love the elderly.
>
> —Betty

From my journal, several months before my fiftieth birthday:

> There's no question that this journal is my therapy. My way of making sense of one more monumental life transition, of finding my way amid all the cacophonous thoughts and feelings that confront me. Of trying to quiet the panic that keeps pushing to the surface, the fear of what might be coming, of illness pain loneliness uselessness death. My way of striking out along another new path, not of changing the ultimate destination, which, I see now, is a fixed, immovable signpost, but of finding a direction that

*will be interesting, and challenging, firm ground, a path
along which I can find something of value, as I have done
before.*

In my late forties I began the journal that became this book. It was my way of comforting myself, of dealing with my anxieties and fears about entering my sixth decade. At the time, I thought I was writing about the event of turning fifty, but that turns out to have been an illusion. What I've really been writing about is the experience of growing through my middle age and approaching my old age as consciously as I can. For all we have, it turns out, is this one life. And if all we do with it is struggle to get from here to there, or, conversely, float through our days without being where we are, doing what we're doing, well, that is a waste.

What I am most interested in is the experience of life, the experience of my life, of yesterday, of today, of tomorrow. And what has become important about middle age is that for the first time I understand something about *how* to experience this one life: Something about how to be, how to reflect, how to learn, how to take risks, how to appreciate, how to participate. How to wonder.

DISCOVERING SPACE AND SOLITUDE

It may be that I am entering a new phase, the simple letting go that means old age. I no longer think, for instance, of buying a piece of furniture or rug ... why add to the things here? (May Sarton, *The House by the Sea: A Journal*)

October 1991. The Oakland Hills fire sweeps through residential districts, devouring home after home. My husband and I watch on television, horrified and fascinated, trying not to think about the tree branches that dangle over our roof. We know it could happen here, that we could lose everything we own in a few hours. It would be the price we pay for living in a forest on the side of Mt. Tamalpais, just as the people who live in the East Bay hills paid for living in wooded splendor with fabulous views of San Francisco Bay. We speculate: What would we save? It's our disaster discussion, the same discussion we'd had two years earlier when the earthquake that struck on the first day of the World Series broke the Bay Bridge and flattened homes in San Francisco's Marina District, the same discussion we had when fires swept Southern California last year and again when an earthquake leveled Kobe, and the Russian River inundated homes in Guerneville and other communities only a few miles north of where we live. Disasters remind us how vulnerable we are.

We've never bothered to catalogue the contents of our house. We have no video to prove the existence of our television, our VCR, our stereo, our "antiques." If it all goes up, or falls down, we'll never be able to remember what we had. I suppose that if disaster does strike, I'll wish we had been more responsible, but honestly, I have no interest in cataloguing anything that can be replaced. During TV coverage of the San Francisco earthquake, I watched a panicked woman in the Marina use her fifteen minutes before the wrecking ball came to throw things like a baby seat out the window to her husband in the street below. I don't mean to be judgmental; maybe she'd already saved the wedding album and baby pictures, and I know that baby seats cost money. But it seemed silly to waste energy salvaging something that could easily be replaced.

So to return to the disaster discussion, what would I save? The dog. The computer disks. As many photographs as I could find. The children's grade school drawings. The cardboard box that holds everything I've ever written. Jennifer's letters from China and her poem, "My Brother Is a Basketball Player," written when she was twelve and Aaron nine. A pair of Aaron's old soccer shoes, the watercolor I bought in Beijing after days of haggling, a few tchotchkies that remind me of special people and special times. Maybe my white linen pants because they fit so well and the black cotton jacket with the patchwork lining that makes me look like a colorful Schmoo. Books, as many as possible. If the rest of it went, I'm not even sure what I'd replace.

Then why do I hold onto so much stuff? What am I willing to do without? We seldom buy furniture or appliances or carpets or linens or lamps unless what we're using breaks or falls apart. We have the requisite TV and VCR and stereo, nothing fancy and easily replaceable. Ditto for kitchenware and linens. We don't go in much for decorative items. We have several tennis racquets. A guitar that is played every day and a piano that hasn't been played in years. Two ancient XT computers and one new Toshiba laptop. A dot matrix printer and a laser printer. A dusty Remington manual typewriter and an even dustier Selectric. The clothes we wear and the clothes we keep in case we might want to wear them someday. Leftover children's clothes and a big green plastic bag filled with tattered stuffed toys. Several radios, some of which work. A large collection of records (but no turntable), which, now that I think of it, should probably go on the "try to save" list. A growing collection of CDs. Books, everywhere. Gardening tools. Piles of suitcases, duffel bags, and backpacks. Board games. Leftover paint. Jars of screws and nuts and washers and picture hooks. Pictures, framed and on the wall, and waiting to be framed and put up on the wall. Boxes of gift wrap and piles of gift boxes. Leftover Christmas cards.

And of course there's the stuff in the basement.

My friend Fran, who is in her sixties, once said, "As I get older, things simply mean less and less." I have to agree. If I weren't a little superstitious, I might speculate that a minor limited controllable disaster would solve the problem of what to do with all those things. As my mind gets more cluttered with ideas and memories and plans, I'm starting to clean out the closets the way I did when I was pregnant. At times, I long to strip the house down and discard all the junk collected haphazardly over the three and a half decades of my grownup life. It's beginning to take on the form of an obsession, this need to throw out or give away everything I do not love that is not essential for survival or at least reasonably comfortable day-to-day living. What is becoming important to me is space and time. I want to start again, and that includes reinventing my environment, stripping down to zip and slowly adding back only things I truly need or truly want because I enjoy looking at them, or touching them, or using them. Things that enrich instead of clutter my life.

It is harder for women perhaps ... to clear space around whatever it is they want to do beyond household chores and family life. Their lives are so fragmented ... the cry is not so much for a "room of one's own" as time of one's own. (May Sarton, *Journal of a Solitude*)

My growing need for uncluttered space is connected to my increasing desire for solitude. I try to arrange my work schedule so I can work at home a day or two a week. I plan those days to coincide with my husband's longest days at the university where he teaches, and I find myself impatient if he isn't out the door early enough to leave me a long stretch of uninterrupted solitude. I'm toying with the idea of taking a cabin or small house somewhere and spending a month or so alone. I envy Margo her three months in Paris on her own. Last week, Fran confided that she's finding her husband's retirement difficult because it's robbed her of the morning solitude she uses to write.

There can be a sense of aloneness that is downright voluptuous, a drawing in, a sense of plenitude and delight. And there is a type of aloneness that is austere, disciplined, not happy yet not unhappy either, usually given at moments when we understand that something difficult has to be faced alone, that a unique life experience can't be shared ... And then there is the ragged, harsh, and inconsolable sense of aloneness that is actually grief, I think, and this is called loneliness. (Dorothy Gilman, *A New Kind of Country*)

I am old enough now to appreciate the difference between solitude and loneliness. It's solitude I have begun to crave, the way I used to crave the company of others. I long for hours alone in a silent house the way I used to long for a Saturday night date.

I still fear loneliness. I hate the anxiety that comes when I am hungry for companionship and no one is available. But I risk loneliness by evading social events and by letting myself get too busy to see my friends or to make new ones. For the first time in my life, my own company is as important to me as the company of others, and I've learned that I can have solitude only if I am willing to accept a measure of loneliness. The question is one of balance.

LOOKING
FORWARD

NEW BEGINNINGS

In any other generation in our history as Americans, what we've done so far would be considered a life's work. Why can't we say, this is our life work, we've done it, we've done a good job, now let's go to the beach. But no. This is my new life I want to start, new challenges, new life work. What I want to know is, how are we going to connect this one with the next one?

—Susan

We've spent so much of our lives trying to figure out what we wanted to be, or what we were supposed to be. Now that we're in our fifties and finally grown up, they tell us we're supposed to be winding down. Whatever the expectations were, you should have met them by now or given them up. You've raised the kids, and they're doing okay, or they're not and there's not a hell of a lot you can do. You've reached the pinnacle of your career, or it's well within your reach, or you've decided not to bother. You've written the novel, or you haven't, and that's that. Tradition says it's time to move aside, rest on our laurels, and make room for the kids. Count down to retirement, and keep our fingers crossed that Social Security and Medicare don't go bankrupt and the money will stretch to cover a condo in Arizona and a few years of travel while we've got the strength to haul suitcases on and off trains. That's the way it's supposed to be. Isn't it?

We in this area and this generation probably have access to a longer period of good health than any other generation in history. There's a greater potential for a longer period of health.

—Lynn

After working hard all their lives, my grandpa and my Zadie retired so they could rest. Not Grandma and Bubba, of course; in those days, women kept on doing what they'd always done, with a lighter workload if they were lucky. My grandparents' retirement was sort of a passive retirement. In those days, retired people didn't replace their everyday activities with something new, they simply stopped doing them. They stayed in the communities in which they'd lived all their lives, unless they moved to be closer to their children. They had time on their hands, so they were available for child care. Grandpa read the newspaper a lot; I'm not sure what else he did with his time. Grandma cooked for Grandpa, cleaned the house, did the laundry, and made dinner for the entire family every Sunday. When Grandma died, Grandpa moved in with my parents. Although I didn't know Bubba and Zadie very well, I imagine that their lives were similar.

My parents' generation transformed themselves, became "senior citizens" instead of old people, and invented "active retirement." With a longer life expectancy than their parents, more money, and more experience with leisure time, they looked forward to retirement as a time for fun; helping raise their beloved grandchildren was not how they defined "fun." In my parents' generation, developers in Florida and Southern California and Arizona found the market for Leisure World and similar adult communities, safe, secure, clean habitats free from the chaos and noise and unpredictability of the young. Retirement redefined as unlimited playtime—golf, tennis, swimming, crafts, Friday night happy hour, and monthly theme parties, with an occasional cruise to break up the routine.

My parents live in such a community in Sonoma, California. It's small as such developments go. There is no gatehouse. There is a thick book of rules. The minimum age is fifty-five (fifty-five!). My parents are among the oldest residents; there is no transitional care facility, so if and when they can no longer care for themselves, they will have to move. But their goal is to remain in their compact two bedroom two bath dining room living room kitchen two car garage home until the end.

A noncommitted, unpassionate existence …
                                        —Susan

I agree. Yet who am I to judge? My parents like it there. They have friends. They feel safe and secure—indeed, they *are* safe and secure. People watch out for one another. When my father was in the hospital, people called every day to see how he was doing and offer my mother rides to Santa Rosa. I may think they're terribly isolated from the real world (whatever that might be), but they don't. The features about the place that I dislike the most—the lack of diversity, the conformity, the rigid rules—allow them security and independence. This community reflects the values that middle-class people of their generation consider important: cleanliness, order, and good manners. Who am I to say they're wrong? After all, I choose to live in a small suburban town where I can walk the streets at night without fear, even though it means isolating myself from the energy and arts and opportunities of the city. What do I know about getting old? It would be foolish for me to say flatly that I will never want the kind of safe, secure, predictable life my parents have found for themselves.

I see so many older people retreat into their little houses and their TV sets and they want everything just so because it's something they can manage. And they're afraid of their frailty, they are very vulnerable, and they are husbanding their energy.

—Lynn

I can see why, when people get older and more frail, they might prefer segregating themselves in carefully structured adults-only communities. As a society, we're not very comfortable with old people. Old people move so slowly. They're so careful and so unattractive. It's much better when they're off the streets, out of sight. We don't want to make concessions to their frailty. We don't want to look at them and be reminded of our mortality.

What have we come to when people are shoveled away, as if that whole life of hard work, dignity, self-respect, could be discarded at the end like an old beer can? (May Sarton, *Journal of a Solitude*)

It would be extreme even to imply that my parents have been "shoveled away." The better term would be "self-segregated." They do not want skateboards and tricycles on their sidewalks or rock music blaring from car radios outside their doors or softball games in the middle of their streets. They are, it seems, just as uncomfortable with younger people as younger people are with them.

From my journal:

I find comfort in routines. Book and snack at bedtime. "Weekend Edition" as I cross the bridge for Sunday morning class. A quiet moment with the newspaper at the end of the day. My own chair at the kitchen table. I resent intrusion. Change.

But I need intrusion. Change.

Perhaps what I find disturbing is how attractive my parents' active retirement sometimes seems. I have already noticed a discord between myself and the more youthful society in which I move. I avoid restaurants where the noise level makes it impossible to have a conversation without shouting across the table. I resent having to jump out of the way when a rollerblader in skin-tight Spandex speeds down the sidewalk or a mountain biker hurtles past me on a narrow trail. I feel out of place in bars and restaurants that cater to people in their twenties and early thirties. My rhythms are different. I move more slowly. I am partial to quiet classical music or good jazz in the background while I dine. But I cringe at the thought of someday retreating into the sterile isolation of an adult community, of settling for my parents' "noncommitted, unpassionate" existence. That's not how I want to envision my as yet undefined future. I know I want something else for myself. Something ...

> *I look forward to the next decade as a big adventure. I feel as if I don't have another chance. Every day is so important. I have just this much time and I want to live it to the fullest. I don't want to fill up my life with extraneous things. I've made decisions in my life that have brought me to where I am right now, to clear the decks so I could pursue my career.*
> —*Sachiko*

Our parents invented their own form of retirement. Why can't we? We might see retirement as an opportunity to stop what we've been doing, the way our grandfathers did, but it doesn't have to be a time to *stop*. Unlike our parents, we're not particularly interested in isolating ourselves from the world, at least not yet. Like them, we also want to have fun, but just as we've defined fun differently for most of our lives, we're defining it differently as we age. Fun might be trying something completely new or going back to something we never let ourselves fully explore. Closing out the law practice and getting a teaching credential. Taking a golden handshake from the corporation and becoming a carpenter. Getting a master's in Creative Writing. Joining the Peace Corps. Studying guitar or acting or painting.

> *When we moved to Arizona, my father was forty-seven. He made a total life change. He gave up his law practice, his entire business in New York. My mother had not even visited Tucson before we moved there. She said, "Why not?" She was forty. To me, the forties and fifties aren't that old. He moved there so he could read and ride and paint. His retirement lasted about two months. Maybe it lasted the ride out there. But that was his intention. New beginnings have always seemed possible to me because of them. It seems like there might be more later than there is before.*
>
> —Margo

My father was a one-career man, a professional musician from the age of fourteen. He made one stab at a midlife career change, buying a bowling alley in partnership with my uncle Harry. Uncle Harry and Aunt Jessie already had one successful bowling alley, the Pico Bowl in Westwood, Los Angeles, and before that had run other successful businesses. They were what we politely referred to as "well-to-do," and I'm sure that my father was looking for financial security not provided by his musical career.

So my parents sold my childhood home for seed money and we moved to a rented house in Redondo Beach. After four weeks of bartending school in Chicago, my father took up his post as manager of the Jola Bowl in Inglewood. It was a courageous, risky move, a big change for my father and mother at an age when people were expected to start slowing down and avoid risks, especially in the Fifties. In the end, it didn't work out. We hated Los Angeles and my father hated the business. One night, we held a dinner table meeting in which we took about two-point-five seconds to decide to pack it in and move back home. My father took a loss on his investment, and I'm sure he took a blow to his ego. But the financial loss and the ego blow were probably worth it. Otherwise my father might never have known that he was a success. Maybe he would never be rich, but he had raised his children and could continue to support himself and his wife in middle-class comfort doing what he loved the most, playing the piano, leading an orchestra, arranging music, coordinating and directing musical events. In a way, my father actually re-created his life by realizing its value. He would be a professional musician for another thirty years before he finally disconnected his business telephone.

> My mother started back to her career as a teacher at the age of fifty. She finally retired when she was seventy- four, so she had twenty-four wonderful years. And my father also went into an entirely new field at the age of fifty. I have a real good feeling about getting old, because other than a few ineffective people in the closets of the family, who were ineffective at the age of twenty, we're long-lived, active, fun, happy people.
>
> —Marlene

> One of the things about getting older that you have to be careful of is to stay in touch. The easiest way is to sit and wait for your kids to bring you news of the outside world,

which is what our grandparents did. Then, if you don't
have a lot of kids, you're in big trouble.

—Leslie

My friend Diane describes people who do nothing as living a kind of death. I guess some people live that way because they don't know what they're supposed to do. It seems as if they're waiting for someone to tell them, but when you tell them they say no, I'm too old, too tired, I don't know how, I can't do that. They never learned that it's okay to make things happen for yourself and okay to try something you've never tried before.

The way to keep from getting old—in the sense that I've always thought of as old, meaning apart, useless, finished—is to keep involved. It doesn't matter what you're involved in. You can tend a garden and show roses. Work in the hospital auxiliary. Run for Congress, perfect your tennis game, go on archeological digs, become a real estate broker, open a restaurant, volunteer as an elementary school aide. From the perspective of the middle of my midlife years, "involved" means remaining active and productive for as long as I can teach a class, pick up a pen, audition for a play, take a walk, or talk with my friends. It means trying to do things I've never done before, challenging myself, and making things happen, even in small ways. Shortly after Martha Graham died, National Public Radio replayed an interview with her conducted when she was nearing or just past ninety. In that interview, she referred to "people who are afraid to walk the razor's edge." That phrase has stayed with me for years. How important it is to walk the razor's edge! To take risks, keep the senses honed, stay alert. To stay fully alive by refusing to sit within the dulling sphere of predictability and safety.

My mother's seventy-eight and really in good shape. She was mostly a housewife, but she's a very independent woman. So many things center around her. She's a focal point. She travels, she's active in the church, you can never catch her at home. You wouldn't think she was seventy-eight, you'd think maybe she was in her sixties.

—Melva

Youth is a kind of genius in itself and knows it. Old age is often expected to recognize that genius and forget its own, so much subtler and gentler, so much wiser. But it is possible to keep the genius of youth into old age, the curiosity, the intense interest in everything from a book to a dog. (May Sarton, *At Seventy: A Journal*)

Middle age, far from heralding the end of life, as I once perceived it to be, is a wonderful time for new beginnings. I no longer care what other people think of me—the only approval I need is my own. I no longer fear failure but welcome it because it brings learning and growth and because I'm no longer as concerned about the outcome as I am about the experience. I face new obstacles—limited time, decreasing energy, the possibility of debilitating illness. But I have so many new resources—knowledge, confidence, sense of self. Everything I've ever done, learned, experienced, or thought about has brought me to this place, and from this place makes it possible for me to move forward.

COMING UP NEXT

I want to leave my mark. I want to participate actively in something important. I want to feel passionately about things. Leave a footprint on Earth that says, "I was here." I guess what I'm doing is preparing the warrior to get out there. I'm off-loading all the nurturing, caretaking stuff, and there's a little bit of regret, but not too much.

—Susan

Do we become more conscious as we grow older? Sometimes it seems as if I've spent most of my life asleep and am just now waking up. It reminds me of the amnesia you get when driving long distances. What—Fresno, already? What—the Nineties, already?

Every minute … I can sit and look at those flowers for five hours and I don't have time to do that because I want to go to French class, and write, and see all my friends, and talk to everybody, and take care of everybody, and go to the cleaners, and get my jewelry fixed, and talk to my dogs, and maybe even work a little bit.

—Margo

From one point of view, it's sad that you learn how to live only when you get close to the end of your life. But a shift of position brings a different point of view: What is the purpose of life if it is not learning how to live? It's like walking through a hall of mirrors. You catch a glimpse of yourself here, turn, it's gone, but out of the corner of your eye … . It's not until you reach the end that you see yourself complete, all the bits mysteriously assembled into one perfect being. Perhaps the single goal is to reach that moment and experience it as fully as possible. To avoid being so distracted by the glimpses along the way that you lose yourself in distorted images or waste precious time backtracking, trying to recapture something you thought you might have had.

From my journal:

> San Francisco, a few weeks after the earthquake that interrupted the World Series. The city shimmers in the sunlight, its wounds well hidden. I love the city energy. I want to move back to this place where I spent my youth, wander the neighborhoods, duck in and out of coffee shops, bookstores. Never cross a bridge. We burn our bridges. Build bridges. Cross bridges when we come to them. I need to build a bridge. From—what? To—what? I am on a bridge, straddling my life, one foot in youth, the other in old age. One in childhood, the other in maturity. Moving towards the far shore, the winter of my life.

Two or three years ago I had a dream—a vision—of myself at the age of ninety-eight or so. I am a tiny white-haired old woman resting on a chaise on a bluff overlooking the sea. The air is warm. My notepad lies in my lap, but I have dropped the pen. My eyes are closed. I listen to the waves wash up on the shore below, and a lifetime of memories washes through my mind. It's as if I have a video camera inside my head, and I can replay moments and images at will. I feel warm and secure and complete. I feel content.

I wish I could get inspiration from a woman who is going through the aging process with grace, with wisdom, accepting limitations, not defying them.

—Vivian

Again I take strength and joy in the friendship of someone older than I … who has made her peace with life and enjoys everything so much … (May Sarton, At Seventy: A Journal)

Creekside Follies, 1993. My seventy-eight-year-old mother has been learning to tap-dance. Stiff and nervous, counting the beats, remember to smile, oops missed a step, sparkley eyelids and strangely tiny and fragile, excited, shimmering. "Was I all right?" she asks in a quivering voice. "I wanted you to think I did a good job." I want to enfold her in my arms. "It's what I always wanted to do, I'm finally doing what I wanted to do," she says. "Did the taps sound all right on the stage, they sounded so wonderful here on the floor, but on the stage … was I all right?"

ABOUT THE AUTHOR

After a stint in the editorial departments of several magazines, including *Ramparts* and *Mother Jones*, Janis Fisher Chan worked as a freelance editor and writer for many years. Since 1980 she has been a partner in a company that provides training services to businesses and publishes self-study business writing books.

Like so many women of her age, she has spent most of her adult life juggling family and work. She ran a theatre company, owned a children's shop, been married to the same man for almost thirty years and raised two children. She has a master's degree in theatre arts from San Francisco State, with postgraduate work in social psychology. She has recently begun to write short stories and plays.

SIBYL PUBLICATIONS

Sibyl Publications is a small press of nonfiction books to empower women. Books are positive, calling forth women's strengths and wisdom. We are dedicated to women's voices being heard.

MYTHMAKING: Heal Your Past, Claim Your Future
Patricia Montgomery, Ph.D.

Discover the power of telling your story and revealing cultural myths. Step-by-step exercises. Thirty myths written by midlife women. "Healing, transformative tool." ISBN 0-9638327-3-5, 224 pages, $14.95, paper.

THE GODDESS SPEAKS: Myths & Meditations
Dee Poth

Book of stories of twenty-five goddesses and set of colorful meditation cards depicting their images, attributes, and meditations. Beautifully packaged for daily use. "Experience the universal feminine." "Meaningful gift." "Uncannily psychic." ISBN 0-9638327-2-7, 120-page book and 25 cards, $29.95 / set.

Journey in the Middle of the Road
Muriel Murch

Vivid account of a midlife woman juggling her life as she returns to school for a nursing degree. "Deeply moving." "Clear, authentic voice!" ISBN 0-9638327-4-3, 200 pages, $16.95, paper.

REDEFINING SUCCESS: Women's Unique Paths
Nancy Johnson

Moving stories of twenty-four remarkable women who discuss their sometimes bumpy paths to success. Striking photographs. "Modern pioneers and an inspiration!" ISBN 0-9638327-5-1, 220 pages, $18.95, paper.

INVENTING OURSELVES AGAIN: Women Face Middle Age
Janis Fisher Chan

Revealing conversations with midlife women about the fears, feelings, and discoveries of aging. "middle age as an adventure." "intimate and engaging, humorous and honest." ISBN 0-9638327-1-9, 210 pages, $14.95, paper.

SACRED MYTHS: Stories of World Religions
Marilyn McFarlane

Sumptuously illustrated oversized book introduces children to seven of the world's religions and enchants them with the sacred stories of each religion. "For the young at heart and the seekers of wisdom." ISBN 0-9638327-3-5, 110 pages, $26.95, hard cover, ages 10 and up.

For more information, call Sibyl Publications, 1-800-240-8566, or write: 600 SE Powell Blvd, Portland, OR 97202